Parenting with Intimacy provides practical, Christ-centered principles for truly "knowing" your ch... ... 1 to "know" you and then ha ...ingly involved in their lives. . .  *1g with Intimacy Workbook* and *In...* ...l are on the cutting edge of eq ...e challenges of the 21st century ...eword).

Josh McDowell

Too often our parental role is relegated in the list of priorities. Excuses, Excuses! *Parenting with Intimacy* reestablishes the vital need to provide time and practical solutions to parenting problems. It reveals how relevant the Scriptures are on the subject. Parents who read this will benefit beyond measure for it will provide them with a blueprint of inestimable value "to their family."

Simon Reading
House of Lords — England

Children are connectors, and if they don't "connect" with their parents, they will connect with their peers. *Parenting with Intimacy* gives the blueprints for parents who want to understand their children's needs and truly stay connected spiritually and emotionally. This is a fine piece of work that will benefit many.

Dennis Rainey, Executive Director
FamilyLife

David and Teresa address the critical issues of family life, parenting, and bonding with an intimacy with Christ, and each member of the family.

This is a very practical book, and a must reading for parents (single parents and couples) and grandparents.

I'm very thankful that the Lord led David and Teresa to write this much needed book, *Parenting with Intimacy*!

Dal Shealy, President/CEO
Fellowship of Christian Athletes

PARENTING WITH INTIMACY

Dr. David & Teresa Ferguson
Dr. Paul & Vicky Warren
& Terri Ferguson

 VICTOR BOOKS

A DIVISION OF SCRIPTURE PRESS PUBLICATIONS INC.
USA CANADA ENGLAND

 INTIMATE
·LIFE·

All Scripture is from the *New American Standard Bible*, © the Lockman Foundation 1960, 1962, 1963, 1968, 1971, 1972, 1973, 1975, 1977.

Editing: Barbara Williams
Design: Scott Rattray

Library of Congress Cataloging-in-Publication Data

Parenting with intimacy / by David & Teresa Ferguson . . . [et al.],
   p. cm.
   ISBN 1-56476-522-9
   1. Parenting—United States. 2. Child rearing—Religious aspects—Christianity. 3. Intimacy (Psychology)—Religious aspects—Christianity. I. Ferguson, David, 1947–
HQ 755.85.P354 1995
248.8'45—dc20
                          95-36977
                          CIP

---

1 2 3 4 5 6 7 8 9 10 Printing/Year 99 98 97 96 95

Dedication

"The land is still ours because we have sought the Lord our God; we sought Him and He has given us rest."
— 2 Chronicles 14:7

Marriages and families are HIS land!

This resource is offered with special dedication to . . .

● The Lord, who *"is intimate with the upright"*
— Proverbs 3:32

● The **Intimate Life** network of churches and other ministries who are colaboring to establish comprehensive, ongoing ministry which deepens intimacy with God, in marriage, family, and the church. While using **Intimate Life** publications and other resources, homes, churches and communities are being "fortified" against such enemies as divorce, abuse, and neglect—providing places of refuge, security, and rest.

"Let the one who is taught the Word share all good things with him who teaches."
— Galatians 6:6

● The **Intimate Life** ministry associates—a network of pastors, ministers, and other Christian leaders who seek to walk intimately with God and with others in their marriages, families, and churches. As these associates faithfully teach the Word, they benefit from specific **Intimate Life** principles and then are able to impart these principles to others. The Galatians 6:6 ministry includes "Intimacy Retreats" and other events for ministry couples in key cities in the United States, the United Kingdom, Europe, and other countries.

For further information on how you might be a part of making an impact on marriages and families in your church or community, contact:

Intimate Life Ministries
P.O. Box 201808
Austin, Texas 78720-1808

Telephone: U.S. 800+881-8008
or 512+795-0498
FAX 512+795-0853
U.K. 080+096-6685

● *Center for Marriage and Family Intimacy* ● *Intimacy Press*
● *Galatians 6:6 Ministry* ● *Intimate Life Communications*
● *Intimacy Institute* ● *Worship Connection*

Contents

Acknowledgments

Countless people have helped shape our contributions to this book. We have learned much from our own families. Our own parents patiently endured our somewhat rebellious journey to grow up, but God brought loving change and healing to these relationships. Even now "Manu," as we all lovingly call David's mom, serves with us in our ministry office.

We have been especially blessed by our three "gifts from the Lord": Terri, Robin, and Eric, plus the recent blessing of our son-in-law, Ike. They have forgiven us as we've failed and join us in frequent times of fun. Now that our nest is empty, they have become the best of blessings— intimate friends!

A special testimony of God's promise to bless us "exceedingly abundant" has been the privilege of working with Terri on this book. Her insight into children and teens is exceeded only by the burden she feels for them.

Significant in our *Intimate Life* message is that "it's not good to be alone." Our special friends, Paul and Vicky Warren, have been faithful partners in this project, removing aloneness and blessing us with the testimony of their burden and hope.

Finally, special thanks to Dave Horton and Victor Books who have patiently supported us as we've field-tested these principles and then encouraged us with their vision for ministry to families.

—David and Teresa Ferguson

Parenting with Intimacy has been a labor of love, and our hearts are filled with gratitude as we pause to reflect on those who labored with us.

First and foremost, thanks be to God who loves us with an everlasting love and forgives us when we falter—which is often! Thank You, Lord, that You're not looking for perfect parents—only faithful ones. "The Lord's lovingkindnesses indeed never cease, For His compassions never fail. They are new every morning; Great is Thy faithfulness" (Lam. 3:22-23).

To our son Matthew—the joy of our lives—for his loving heart and forgiving spirit . . . and for his willingness to allow us to share our family with you—"warts and all"—in the hope that you will be encouraged to join us in this journey of parenting with intimacy.

To our families and friends for their love, support, and sustaining prayers.

To David and Teresa Ferguson, our friends and coauthors, for their love and support, for their example, and for inviting us to minister with them as part of the Intimate Life team.

To Terri Ferguson—for her friendship, creativity, sense of humor, and love for kids.

And, finally, to David Horton and Victor Books—Thank you for catching the Intimate Life vision and for believing in his project.

We feel blessed to be part of this project and pray that your hearts will be blessed as you embark on your journey of "parenting with intimacy."

—Paul and Vicky Warren

My heartfelt thanks goes to Paul and Vicky Warren for the privilege of joining them on this book writing journey. It has been a tremendous blessing to see and hear the love of Christ flow through their lives. I appreciate their giftedness and sincere desire to serve others, but most of all I appreciate the "realness" about their lives.

Very few children get the chance to write a book with their parents, but I have had that special joy. Thank you Mom and Dad for your willingness to make an impact on the lives of parents and families. Thank you for your willingness to make an impact on my life. Robin, Eric and I have indeed been given an intimacy heritage.

—Terri Ferguson

Foreword

"Unless the Lord builds the house, they labor in vain who build it. . . . " —Psalm 127:1.

It's sobering, but true. Only two kinds of homes are being built—those the Lord builds and those being built in vain.

As you begin this study, get ready for a radically different approach to parenting. A different approach than "the 10 latest tips to get kids to behave." This book, along with the *Parenting with Intimacy Workbook* and *Intimate Family Moments* devotional are on the cutting edge of equipping homes to withstand the challenges of the 21st century.

Biblically sound and relationally relevant, parents are challenged to impart not only the Gospel, "but their very lives" (1 Thes. 2:8). With suggested exercises and family night activities, homes are being fortified against attack—providing places of refuge and security.

The New Testament admonishes parents to "provoke not children to wrath" (Eph. 6:4) and there may be no quicker way to provoke wrath in a child than for parents to discipline a child they *do not even know! Parenting with Intimacy* provides practical, Christ-centered principles for truly "knowing" your children, allowing them to "know" you and then hands-on exercises to become caringly involved in their lives. These intimacy ingredients are blended together to establish an "intimacy heritage." One day when your child reflects on "how did I know my parents truly loved me," they'll boldly declare:

- through the undivided attention they gave me
- through their patient listening to my hurts and fears
- through their example of faith, conviction, and prayerful walk

- through their empathy and openness as we shared feelings
- through their valuing my thoughts and opinions
- through their trust of my decisions and plans
- through the common interests and fun we shared
- through their verbalized appreciation and love
- through their openness to touch, hug, and reassurance just with their presence.

Congratulations to the Ferguson-Warren team and *Intimate Life Ministries* as they see ongoing marriage and family ministries established within the church.

May God richly bless your journey through these pages as you deepen your intimacy with Him and with your children as "gifts from the Lord" — Psalm 127:3.

"The land is still ours because we have sought the Lord our God" — 2 Chronicles 14:7. Marriages and families are HIS land!

—Josh McDowell

CHAPTER 1

Understanding Intimacy Needs

AS YOU LOOKED at the many books on parenting lining the bookstore shelf, what intrigued you about *Parenting with Intimacy* to the point that you purchased it in lieu of your many other options? Were you hoping to get this year's "Top Ten Tips for Shaping up Your Kids"? If so, you may want to beat a hasty retreat to the bookstore while their return policy is still in force because we'll be asking you to dig deeper. Although an important aspect of parenting, discipline is not the number-one issue. Truly knowing your child, allowing yourself to be known by him, and becoming caringly involved are the keys that will unlock their hearts and minds. Loving your child is not a feeling—it's an action! You're about to take action as you embark on an exploration of a new dimension of parenting—parenting with intimacy.

Several years ago, parents everywhere responded with a heartfelt "Amen!" to Dr. James Dobson's book entitled *Parenting Isn't for Cowards.* Isn't that the truth! Likewise, parenting with intimacy is not for the fainthearted, weak-kneed, or self-centered. Congratulations on having the courage to join us.

No one has parenting "figured out." We're all fellow-sojourners on this journey. Some may be a little farther along, but we're all still works-in-progress. As authors, it would be ego-enhancing to let you believe that we have arrived. Ego-enhancing—decidedly; dishonest—definitely! It's been said that confession is good for the soul but bad for the reputation. Be that as it may, we want you to know that we've made mistakes—lots of them! Throughout the ensuing pages, we'll share some of the true-life "Adventures in Parenting" of the Warrens and the Fergusons. Up close and personal. Meet your traveling companions: The Warrens—Paul, Vicky, and Matthew . . . and the Fergusons—David, Teresa, Terri, Robin, and Eric. And we wouldn't want to forget Ike—Robin's husband of two years. Ready? Then let's get started. Indiana Jones, eat your heart out! You only thought you'd cornered the market on adventure.

Born Needy

We all come into this world needy, whether we want to admit it or not. God created each of us with physical, emotional, and spiritual needs. How those needs are met or go unmet will affect our behavior and view of ourselves and the world around us. Unfortunately, in our pull-yourself-up-by-your-bootstraps society, "neediness" conjures up visions of weakness and dependency. Horror of horrors that we should be dependent on anyone! But let's reason this out. If you're born needing something, are you selfish or weak because you need it? Think about it. Not too many people apologize for their physical needs. "I'm sorry to be using up so much air. I know it's selfish of me, but I just have this need to breathe." Sounds ridiculous, doesn't it? But many of us tend to feel guilty for having intimacy needs and conclude we must be flawed in some way.

How could the Apostle Paul state confidently in Philippians 4:19, "And my God shall supply all your needs according to His riches in glory in Christ Jesus" if we're not supposed to have needs? Gotcha! The verse makes no sense apart from the reality that we all have needs that were placed within us by our Creator.

Need convincing? (Men usually do!) Let's travel all the way back to the Garden of Eden. In Genesis 2 we find Adam in a perfect world—at "the top of his game," to put it in today's vernacular. He had it all—or so it seemed.

Then God appeared on the scene, looked at Adam and said something He'd never said before. "It's not good." Adam had a need he didn't even know he had! He was alone. God ministered to Adam's aloneness by giving him Eve. Two things to ponder here:

• God created Adam, so his aloneness and subsequent need for companionship were no accident, flaw in design, or sin.

• God met Adam's need through Eve.

Conclusions:

• It must be OK to have needs.

• It must be OK (and, in fact, important to God) to have our needs met.

• God is at work to meet our needs—through Himself and through others.

• God can be trusted to meet our needs—challenging us to exercise faith.

• God seeks to involve us in giving to the needs of others—out of the abundance of His provision for us.

These conclusions begin to give insight into establishing and maintaining intimate relationships. Intimate relationships involve a deep "knowing" of another person—just as God saw the inner aloneness of Adam; and they require caring involvement at the point of need—just as God ministered to Adam's need. So, as we begin our journey in parenting with intimacy, we will be challenged to truly *know* our child and become caringly involved in giving to his needs.

Why would we deem it necessary to lay this groundwork? It's essential because an attitude of *self-reliance* and *self-sufficiency* is a guaranteed road hazard that will stop you dead in your tracks in your quest for intimate relationships, especially with your kids. This mind-set says, "I don't need anything or anybody. Or, if I do need anything I'll take care of it myself." Unfortunately, there's a certain degree of pressure in Christian circles today to exalt self-reliance and equate it with maturity. The message is, "If you were just spiritual enough and mature enough in your faith you wouldn't have needs. The fact that you do indicates there must be something wrong with you. If you were really spiritual, all you would need is Jesus." Really? Adam had God, and God said, "It's not good." He wanted more for Adam.

If as parents we project an air of self-reliance and self-sufficiency, it will be impossible to be sensitive to the needs of our children. An attitude will spill over to them that says, "What's wrong with you? Why don't you just grow out of that?" For years the National Dairy Council had as their advertising catchphrase, "You never outgrow your need for milk." May we suggest a slight variation — *You never outgrow your needs.* It would be ludicrous to expect that you could just fill your lungs with oxygen once and have a sufficient air supply to last you a lifetime. What a time saver that would be! Your need to breathe taken care of once-for-all! One less thing to have to do every day. Sounds ridiculous, doesn't it! On an emotional level, does it sound reasonable that a parent could meet her child's need for, let's say affection, on a one-shot basis? Intimacy needs are met on an ongoing basis and must be constantly replenished.

Why did God create us with needs anyway? To answer that, we must first establish that we can't meet our own needs. Uh, oh. We're stepping on toes already. Most of us delude ourselves into thinking that we actually do provide for our own physical needs and those of our families. However, if we were to backtrack to the beginning of the trail, we would see that God the Creator and Sustainer of everything is actually doing the providing.

We are equally incapable of meeting our own intimacy needs. The last time you experienced discouragement or disappointment who or what ministered to your need for encouragement? Did you seek solace from your reflection in the bathroom mirror? Or, did you receive a reassuring hug or understanding word from a meaningful person in your life? God does not intend for us to be lone rangers. Self-talk works to a point, but by virtue of its very meaning, "intimacy" needs must be met through relationships. Our needs are what stimulate our faith as we look beyond ourselves and allow God to lovingly meet our needs through both our vertical relationship with Him and our horizontal relationships with meaningful others—in marriage, the family, and the church. We short-circuit this process when we deny the existence of our needs.

Our attempts to avoid taking an honest "needs inventory" is more than likely motivated by our fear of what we might find. Even more frightening for many parents is the prospect of discovering how they may have "messed up" their kids. Know what? Mistakes don't hurt kids irreparably—attitudes do. The potential destructiveness of an attitude of self-reliance has already been addressed. Just as devastating is the attitude that says, "Ignorance is bliss. What I don't know can't hurt me or my kids." Wrong!

John 8:32 says, "And you shall know the truth, and the truth shall make you free." It's true that we have all been "undernourished" in some areas of need. Unmet needs are inevitable as we grow up in an imperfect world—as imperfect children—with imperfect parents—in imperfect families. Healthy/functional families deal with the hurt of unmet needs while unhealthy/dysfunctional families deny the hurts, ignore the needs, and/or look for someone to blame.

So, let's take off the blinders or rose-colored glasses and commit to looking honestly at ourselves and our children in order that we may know each other intimately. In order to know your children, you'll have to look inside.

Unwrapping the Gift

One of the most important investments a parent can make in the lives of their children is to *know* them. Psalm 127:3 says, "Behold, children are a gift from the Lord." Imagine being presented with an exquisitely wrapped package. You receive it graciously and proceed to carefully place it on the shelf. Six months later the giver returns to your home and is disheartened upon observing that the gift has remained unopened all that time. What would be the logical conclusion? You're uninterested and unappreciative. You've taken the gift—and the giver—for granted. You've missed a tremendous blessing. What a waste!

An integral part of this journey of parenting with intimacy is taking your child—your gift—and untying the bow, undoing the wrapping, and enjoying and getting to know this child deeply, intimately. Unwrap your gift carefully, with a sense of awe. Appreciate each stage of the unveiling because each layer is important and reveals clues about the treasure that lies within.

A crucial step in this process is understanding your child's "intimacy needs" and how these affect his behavior. Remember bringing your newborn home from the hospital? It wasn't long before you realized that little bundle needed more than just air, food, and water. Baby's cry often signaled a different type of need: "Mommy/Daddy, I need to be held, rocked, cuddled. I need attention. I need to be comforted."

Our intimacy needs cry out for someone to be attentive, take the initiative, and become caringly involved. Here is a list of ten of the most important intimacy needs we all have. As we explore these, we'll try to address one of David's [Ferguson] favorite queries, "What does that look like?" in the nitty-gritty of everyday family life.

Attention

To take thought of another and convey appropriate care, interest, concern, and support; to enter into another's world (see 1 Cor. 12:25).

Whatever their age, it's impossible to meet your children's need for attention without entering their world and investing the valuable commodity of T-I-M-E. Several years ago a study was released that documented that the average father in America was spending fourteen minutes a week one-on-one with his children. Fourteen minutes a week! Sadly, ten of those were spent in discipline. In many ways we are raising a generation of children whose only concept of a father is a person they do not know and who does not know them, entering their lives mainly to discipline them. Ephesians 6:4 admonishes fathers not to provoke their children to wrath. We would submit to you that one of the quickest ways to provoke children to wrath is to be a stranger trying to discipline them. It's impossible to know your children without spending time with them, without entering into *their* world.

Jesus gave us the perfect example of this when He chose to give up His position in heaven and entered into our world so that He could know us and we could know Him. As parents, we are similarly challenged to leave our adult world of work, career, hobbies, ministry, and friends to enter into a child's world:

—a world of make-believe, stories, and toys
—a world of play, silly games, and laughter
—a world of technology, thrill-seeking, and heartaches
—a world of disappointment, "strange music," and insecurities

Acceptance

Deliberate and ready reception with favorable positive response; to receive willingly; to regard as good and proper (see Rom. 15:7).

"Don't insist that everything about me be like you—or anyone else. Accept me as significant, unique, and loved, in spite of my behavior. Don't equate my *worth* to you with my 'performance.' Demonstrate your love toward me 'while I'm yet a sinner!' (Rom. 5:8)"

Approval

To accept as satisfactory; to give formal or official sanction to; to have or express a favorable opinion; to approve of (see Rom. 14:18).

Three-year-old Bobby ran into his daddy's study, proudly clutching his first finger painting attempt.

"Daddy, Daddy! Look what I did today in preschool."

Suppose he receives this response, "Not now, Bobby. Can't you see I'm busy!"

Rather than receiving acceptance and approval, Bobby feels rejection. As he walks dejectedly back to his room, his need for approval unmet, he may be *thinking*, "What's wrong with me? I must not be important." Or, "I'll try harder next time. It's my fault. If I'd done a better job, Daddy would've wanted to see it." What kinds of *feelings* might Bobby have? Hurt. Rejection. Anger. Loneliness. What might Bobby's *behavior* be like when he gets back to his room? Color on the walls? Tear up his picture and throw it in the trash? Pull the cat's tail? Pinch his baby sister?

This is the origin of many unhealthy thinking patterns, or "cognitive distortions," that sow the seeds for problems later in life. When experienced consistently over a long period of time, this type of "There must be something wrong with me" thinking may lead to insecurity, feelings of inadequacy, and depression. Thoughts of "I'll try harder. I'll do better," feed into a life characterized by drivenness, workaholism, and perfectionism. The diagram on page 21 may help you visualize this process.

"Aren't you being a little hard on Bobby's dad?" you may be asking. "Maybe he had a deadline and just didn't have time right then. It happens! Lighten up on the guy."

We're not advocating a child must have instant gratification. In fact, learning to delay gratification is an important milestone on the way to maturity. Assuming Bobby's dad did have a pressing deadline and couldn't give Bobby the attention he was seeking, he could still have affirmed Bobby's need with a caring commitment to meet it later.

"Pal, I can see you're really excited about your picture. Tell you what. I need about thirty minutes to finish this report, and then when I'm finished I'll come to your room and you can tell me about your picture and about what you did at school today. Then we'll hang your picture on the refrigerator door so Mommy and baby sister can enjoy it too." He follows that up with a hug and Bobby leaves the room feeling affirmed and loved. What a difference!

Appreciation

To recognize with gratitude; to communicate with words and feeling personal gratefulness for another person; to praise (see 1 Cor. 11:2).

UNDERSTANDING INTIMACY NEEDS

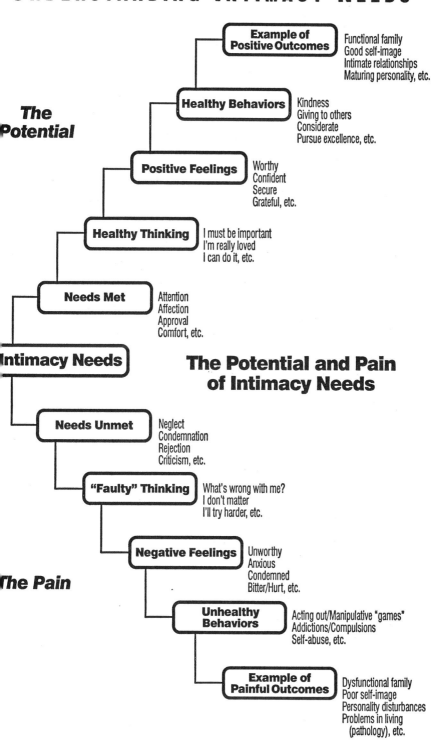

The Potential

Example of Positive Outcomes
Functional family
Good self-image
Intimate relationships
Maturing personality, etc.

Healthy Behaviors
Kindness
Giving to others
Considerate
Pursue excellence, etc.

Positive Feelings
Worthy
Confident
Secure
Grateful, etc.

Healthy Thinking
I must be important
I'm really loved
I can do it, etc.

Needs Met
Attention
Affection
Approval
Comfort, etc.

Intimacy Needs

The Potential and Pain of Intimacy Needs

Needs Unmet
Neglect
Condemnation
Rejection
Criticism, etc.

"Faulty" Thinking
What's wrong with me?
I don't matter
I'll try harder, etc.

Negative Feelings
Unworthy
Anxious
Condemned
Bitter/Hurt, etc.

The Pain

Unhealthy Behaviors
Acting out/Manipulative "games"
Addictions/Compulsions
Self-abuse, etc.

Example of Painful Outcomes
Dysfunctional family
Poor self-image
Personality disturbances
Problems in living
    (pathology), etc.

Meeting this need for appreciation requires thought and effort by parents because the seemingly endless demands on a parent's time and energy make it easier to focus on correcting their kids than looking for ways to express appreciation. This is not to say that misbehavior does not need to be addressed and dealt with appropriately, but kids need to hear an occasional "Well done!" and "Thank you" when appropriate choices are made. No parent wants to feel taken for granted. Kids are no different!

"I really appreciate the way you took care of your younger brother this afternoon. I know you had other things you could have done with your friends that would have been more fun. You're a great big brother."

"I've noticed how much effort you've been putting into keeping your room picked up this week. I really appreciate your helpfulness. It feels great that we're all a team."

Support/Bear Burden

To come alongside and gently help carry a problem or struggle; to assist; to provide for (see Gal. 6:2).

Kids need a journeymate who will walk alongside them to navigate the road hazards on their path toward maturity. This does not mean shouldering the load for them. In the long run, doing so would actually be a hindrance rather than help because it would convey the message, "This is too scary, too difficult for you. You'd better stand aside while I take over." It also does not mean standing at a distance while your child struggles alone. Rather, offering support involves conveying both through words and actions that you're there for your child—no matter what. Looking down the road toward maturity can be a frightening prospect. Your child needs to know he won't be traveling alone.

Encouragement

To urge forward and positively toward a goal; to inspire with courage, spirit, or hope; to stimulate unto love and good deeds (see 1 Thes. 5:11).

All children need a fan club. Knowing that Mom and Dad are cheering them on provides a tremendous impetus to propel them toward reaching for a goal. Mom and Dad, you'll have to deal with the natural tendency to want to shield your children from failure and disappointment. Give them your wholehearted blessing to reach for the sky.

Peter had wanted to be on the varsity wrestling team since he was in sixth grade. Although Peter had never been a "super jock," his parents had encouraged him to go for it. Through dogged determination and rigorous training, Peter realized his dream. On the day of his first wrestling tournament, Jim and Sandy sent their son off to do battle with memories of months of encouragement. There were the obvious heart-to-heart conversations where Jim and Sandy were there to spur him on even when he was discouraged. But there were also the "You can do it!" notes his mom left on the refrigerator and the "Son, you're the greatest in my book!" note his dad left on the dashboard of Peter's car the morning he tried out for the team. And, of course, there were the two most important people in his life cheering him on from the stands the day of the tryouts!

Affection

To communicate care and closeness through physical touch and affirming words (see Rom. 16:16).

Affection is not that mysterious. Affection is looking into your child's eyes, opening your mouth, and verbalizing your love. "I really love you!" It's giving hugs and kisses. Little children run around with their arms out wanting to be hugged. "Hold me. Cuddle me. Rock me. Touch me." As kids grow older, it becomes "uncool" to admit one's need for these things, but the need is there nonetheless. Affection is offered in age-appropriate ways and doses. Parents can be tempted to reduce their affection as kids seem not to "enjoy" it; resist this temptation. Verbalize your love at times of "celebration" and disappointment. Notes of loving care are great for teenagers. Continue to show affection through touch and hugs—even if they're going through a stage where they don't hug back.

Security

Freedom from exposure to danger; to put beyond hazard of losing, want, or deprivation; confidence of "harmony" in relationships (see Ps. 122:6).

The world is a scary place to live, especially if you're a kid. Violence, destruction, danger are all around and are constantly portrayed in the media. All kids, as they grow up, will know of families that are being torn apart by divorce, violence, drugs, and/or abuse; and that brings added worries and fears. Your child needs to know that even though your family goes through tough times, you are committed to one another and to working problems out together.

It might be as simple as a dad verbalizing at the dinner table, "Kids, I was just thinking today about how special your mom is—I'm sure glad she's my wife!" (As Dad kisses Mom, the kids are blessed by the security of their commitment. This declaration of love "casts out fear" (1 John 4:18-19).

It might be a single parent declaring, "I know we've been through some challenging times, but I want you to know that I'm more committed than ever to love, protect, and comfort you."

Although they'll deny it until the bitter end, in order to have a sense of security, kids need to know where the limits are and that there is someone in their lives who cares enough to enforce the limits through loving discipline. Disciplining your child is thus seen in the context of ministering to their need for security. Don't hold your breath waiting for them to thank you, but be confident that you are, indeed, meeting one of their deepest needs.

Comfort

To come alongside with word, feeling, and touch to ease the grief or pain; to console or cheer (see 2 Cor. 1:3-4).

Sit on a bench in any playground and you'll observe a perfect example of a child's need for comfort. When a child falls down, they look around to see if anyone's watching. If they find an empathetic witness to their plight, they say, "No big deal!" and go right back to playing. Hardly! They pucker up and open the floodgates. If the observer happens to be a loved one, the child will usually rush into their arms for a hug, some cuddling, and a kiss to "make it all better." The message is received, "I'm sorry you're hurting. I'm here for you."

The need for comfort for emotional wounds is just as intense.

When Lucy's mom picked her up from school, Lucy's dress was torn, her knees skinned, and her cheeks streaked with tears. "Lucy, sweetheart, what's wrong?" her mother asked. So far, so good. Haltingly, in between sobs, Lucy replied, "Sarah pushed me down on the playground and called me a name in front of all my friends." Right now Lucy needs to hear something along the lines of, "Honey, I know how much that must have hurt your feelings. I'm sorry that happened, and I feel sad that you're sad." Instead, what she heard was, "Well, what did you do to make her do that?" Instead of comfort, she received shame, blame, and condemnation.

It's a paradox. When loved ones are hurting they don't need what we seem inclined to give: facts, logic, advice, criticism. What they do need is *comfort:* an emotional expression that we care—weeping with those who weep, comforting those who mourn.

Respect

To value and regard highly; to convey great worth to; to esteem (see 1 Peter 2:17).

The need for respect is not something that magically appears when a person turns twenty-one. We all need respect—from day one. Children, while God-given gifts to their family, are their own person. They're on loan from God, and He has a special, unique plan for each of them.

Part of meeting your children's need for respect is recognizing that their strengths and weaknesses are part of their unique design and not trying to remold them according to your blueprint.

Children need to experience respect in three distinct areas: their feelings, their opinions, and their possessions. They need to hear from their parents:

"I'm listening. Your thoughts and feelings are very important to me."

"I understand your need to be alone sometimes."

"I understand your need for privacy and your need to have things that belong to you."

"God made you just the way He wanted you. No mistakes. No accidents. And I think you're a terrific kid!"

Keeping Your Eyes and Ears Open

God created each of us unique and special. While it's true that we all have the same needs, the priority or hierarchy of our needs is different. Within your family, for instance, *attention* may be at the top of your list while your spouse's greatest need is *approval*. One child may need megadoses of *encouragement*, but your other child craves *affection*. Have your antennae up and your eyes and ears open. Opportunities to minister to your child's needs may come when you least expect them—and often at the most inopportune times. Consider . . .

. . . The Case of the Soccer Ball-Eating Tree . . .

We told you up front we've made lots of mistakes . . . but, we've gotten it right too! Let's look at an "Adventure in Parenting" scenario compliments of the Ferguson clan.

One steamy Sunday afternoon, six-year-old Eric burst through the back door. "Dad! Dad! Remember that Peanuts cartoon where there was a kite-eating tree?"

David looked up from the outline he was preparing for his parenting class at church that evening. "Yes, Eric, I remember."

"Well, Dad. We have a soccer ball-eating tree in our backyard! It ate my ball and won't give it back! We need to go outside and get it out!"

Eric needed David's attention. For a fleeting moment David entertained the thought, "Not now, Eric. Can't you see I'm busy preparing for my parenting class?" Laughing to himself at the irony of it all, David took Eric's hand and they headed off to confront the Goliath-like cottonwood tree that had devoured Eric's ball.

The tree was humongous! Their only hope was to throw something into the tree to knock it loose. For the next hour they used every available means to get that stubborn, stingy old tree to cough up the ball. At one point, the tree was the proud owner of not just the soccer ball but a tennis ball, a tennis racket, a baseball, a baseball bat, and a garden hose.

As David pitched each item at the entrenched soccer ball, Eric coached gleefully from the sidelines, "No, Dad. Too far to the left. More to the right. Almost, Dad. Too high. Too low. Try again!"

Finally, persistence paid off. Eric's ball was rescued. Father and son stood victorious. Drenched with perspiration, but victorious nonetheless. Where was the victory? In the retrieved ball? No, a higher victory had been gained that afternoon. Eric had expressed a need, and David entered into Eric's world to meet his need. As a result, Eric's *thinking* process may have been something like this.

- "I must be important."
- "Dad must really care about me to come out here and play with me even when he was busy."
- "Dad must really love me to want to spend time with me like that."

Thinking affects feelings. ("As a man thinks in his heart, so is he.") Eric *feels* loved, secure, hopeful, important, significant. Thinking/feeling affect behavior.

As they stood triumphantly in the backyard, Eric threw his arms around David and said, "Thanks, Dad!" That altruistic, giving *behavior* sprang from a grateful heart. Eric had freely received and was prompted to freely give (Matt. 10:8).

If Any of You Lacks Wisdom

Parenting with intimacy is an awesome calling. As you begin your journey, ask the Lord for wisdom. He promises in James 1:5 to give it generously and without reproach. He knows we need Him and is just waiting for us to invite Him to be our constant companion and omniscient guide. He's the only One who knows what lies ahead. He knows every bend and curve in the road, every pothole, every detour. Don't start your journey without Him.

> *But if any of you lacks wisdom, let him ask of God,*
> *who gives to all men generously and without reproach,*
> *and it will be given to him.*
>
> *James 1:5*

Ask Yourself

1. It is usually quite easy to view a newborn or young child as "needy." We are comfortable with their need for attention, affection, or comfort. Why do we tend to change this view as a child becomes school-aged? An adolescent? An adult?

2. God could have created us without needs — with no need for food, water, attention, affection, etc. Why do you think He chose to create us with needs? How might our neediness relate to our faith, humility, or trust?

Experiencing Truth

1. Acts 20:35 says, "It is more blessed to give than to receive." With this in mind, review the list of intimacy needs. What needs would each of your children most enjoy receiving? What about your spouse? Don't discuss it with them; just begin giving. Meet this need consistently and joyfully this week. Then keep a journal of the blessings *you* receive from giving.

2. Ephesians 4:29 tells us to speak "only such a word as is

good for edification, according to the *need* of the moment."
Practice this verse as you relate to your spouse and your children this week. Discern their need before you speak. Review the list of intimacy needs and look for opportunities to meet the "need of the moment." For example:

You're doing a great job of keeping your room cleaned up. (Appreciation)

I would really like to play with you. As soon as we finish dinner, how would you like to play Battleship? (Attention)

Special Thoughts for Single Parents

As a single parent, be sure to replenish your emotional "bank account." Stay involved in positive adult activities, support networks, and Christ-centered friendships. Maintaining these relationships will allow God to minister to you and your needs. Keeping your emotional resources at an optimum level will enable you to continue giving lovingly to your children.

Special Thoughts for Blended Families

Prioritize your marriage relationship, then give to your children. There's a normal but mistaken tendency to try to compensate for a broken home by prioritizing the children. Children from divorced homes experience the loss of security that results when an adult man and woman cease to sacrificially and permanently love one another. As a blended family you now have the opportunity to minister to this loss by reaffirming the secure relationship between married partners. Make it a priority to meet your spouse's intimacy needs.

CHAPTER 2

God's Plan for Growing Up

YOU'VE BARELY PULLED away from the driveway and the incessant clamor from the backseat begins. "Are we there yet?" "How much farther?" "When will we get there?" "She's touching me." "He's bothering me." "Tell her to stop looking at me." "She's on my side. Tell her to move." Sounds all too familiar, doesn't it! It's the predictable background music every parent listens to (endures!) on family trips as they ask themselves, "Are we having fun yet?"

Interestingly enough, kids aren't the only ones asking, "Are we there yet?" Beleaguered parents often echo those same sentiments as they search for the energy to press on. Fueled by America's belief that faster equals better, we're to the point that a three-minute wait for the microwave to deliver a completely cooked meal seems torturous. And, if faster equals better, instant must equal best! Nothing could be farther from the truth when it comes to rearing our children. It takes time—and lots of it.

As is true of our attitude toward so much of what God has put here for us to enjoy and appreciate, we have tended to devalue childhood in our society. We tell our kids with our words and actions to "Hurry up and grow up." The underlying message is that their importance is found in what they will become—*when* they finish school, *when* they get their degree, *when* they get a good-paying job, *when* they marry the right person, *when* they have a family of their own. There's a Greek word that defines this attitude—*hogwash!* They are important *NOW*—not when.

God's plan for growing up is one of His most intricate creations—exciting and scary, exhilarating and tiring, rewarding and frustrating, all-too-short and endless—all at the same time. The developmental milestones, or watershed events, that must occur at various ages along God's appointed timetable are extremely important. Nobody ever grew up to be a healthy, mature adult by avoiding them. It's natural for a parent to want to shield their child from some of the painful moments encountered along the way, but learning to negotiate the roadblocks and detours is critical to completion of the journey. If a child doesn't deal with the issues of being twelve when she's twelve, she'll have to deal with them later—at twenty, twenty-five, thirty-five, forty-five . . .

Remember, things take time. Growing up is no exception! Also remember that critical to relating *intimately* with your child is to truly know her—and a good place to start is knowing about kids and God's plan for their growing up. What is the universal parental response to that irritating backseat inquiry, "Are we there yet?" Altogether now . . . "Not yet. Just sit back and enjoy the scenery!" So, let's commit to practicing what we preach. Enjoy watching the panorama of your child's life as it unfolds frame-by-frame, according to God's timetable. God has created and ordained the process of growing up. Every moment of every day is incredibly important and brings an opportunity for building relationships. Gaining an understanding of the orderly progression of stages God has preordained for our children to pass through enables us to be more empathetic and equips us to help them discover their uniqueness and God-given potential. Let's begin.

Designer Genes

Your child's developmental journey began long before his or her eyes first beheld the glaring lights of the delivery room. Psalm 139 offers a beautiful confirmation of the fact that God was actively at work not only while baby was in the womb but even before conception.

For Thou didst form my inward parts;
Thou didst weave me in my mother's womb.
I will give thanks to Thee, for I am fearfully and
wonderfully made;
Wonderful are Thy works.
And my soul knows it very well.
My frame was not hidden from Thee,
When I was made in secret,
And skillfully wrought in the depths of the earth.
Thine eyes have seen my unformed substance;
And in Thy book they were all written,
The days that were ordained for me,
When as yet there was not one of them.

(Ps. 139:13-16)

God loves variety. Blond hair, blue eyes. Brown hair, brown eyes. Red hair, green eyes. Tall, short, and in between. "Red and yellow, black and white . . . They are precious in His sight." These verses assure us that we were each created by the Master Designer, according to plan—no miscalculations, no mistakes. In a sense, we all made our grand entrance into this world wearing Designer genes!

These Designer genes imprint more than just our physical characteristics. Temperament is, for the most part, genetically determined as well. Webster defines temperament as "the characteristic physiological and emotional state of an individual, which tends to condition his responses to the various situations of life." In other words, it's how we're wired together. Some kids, for example, are extremely adaptable. They're very laid back. No matter what happens, it just kind of rolls off. Change is no big deal. Then there are those kids who go to pieces over the least little variation of their routine. Change sends them into a tailspin that often results in a crash landing.

Another temperament characteristic is rhythmicity. This has nothing to do with whether they'll be the next Ginger Rogers or Fred Astaire. It's how their day-to-day internal biological cycles are set. Some babies sleep calmly all night and are awake all day. Others sleep all day and are awake all night. These patterns tend to stay with a person throughout life. Witness the existence of "morning people" and "night people."

A child's activity level is another example. Some kids seem to have minds, mouths, and motors that are constantly moving. Others tend to lean more toward being couch potatoes. Some kids are born shaking hands—extroverts from day one. Others are more introverted—shy and reserved.

While parents can mold, shape, and direct, they cannot change a child's God-given design and, in fact, shouldn't try—as inconvenient as it may make life at times. And yet, parents frequently attempt to do just that. Sometimes their efforts are subtle and other times they are as blatant as saying, "Why can't you be more like Sarah? She always sits quietly and never says a word." Or, "Why can't you be more like Johnny? He takes naps like he's supposed to and doesn't argue with his mommy all the time." This "Why can't you be more like _____" message sets in motion negative thought processes such as, "There must be something wrong with me. I'll try harder. I'll do better." The child's need for approval and respect are left unmet, leaving her wide open for feelings of hurt, rejection, and anger. And, as we've seen, negative thoughts and feelings result in unproductive behavior.

Ephesians 2:10 says, "For we are His workmanship, created in Christ Jesus for good works, which God prepared beforehand, that we should walk in them." That word *workmanship* actually comes from a Greek word that means poetry. So, in essence, we are God's poetry. He has made each child unique—exactly as He wanted. Follow His lead. Rather than trying to change God's rhythm and rhyme, develop an appreciation and acceptance for the poem He has entrusted to your care.

Who Do You Trust? Or Do You? (Infancy)

In the not-so-distant past, it was thought that newborns just needed to be held, fed, burped, changed, and put to bed. We have since learned that infancy is an incredibly active time. Amazing things are happening. Moment-to-moment, hour-to-hour, day-to-day, this infant is learning a fundamental lesson that will determine the quality of the foundation upon which all future relationships are built. As baby's intimacy needs are either met by caring adults or remain unmet, the question is answered, "Can relationships be trusted?" It's not a matter of whether or not you will teach them about trust... it's *what* will you teach them.

If we could get inside a newborn's thought processes, we would hear something like this. "When I'm hungry, my mommy feeds me. Daddy does too sometimes. They hold me. They change me when I'm wet. They talk to me and sing to me. Daddy lets me pull his whiskers. When I cry they come to see what's wrong. They rock me and pat me on the back. I can trust Mommy and Daddy to love me and take care of me."

We see the flip side of this all around us in news reports every day. A growing number of babies are learning quite the opposite lesson about trust. Instead of having their needs met by loving, caring adults, they are neglected, abandoned, or abused. Crawling inside this infant's head we would hear, "When I'm hungry no one comes. When I cry because I'm wet, I'm punished. When I need to be comforted, I'm ignored. The world is an unsafe place. Since I can't trust anyone else to meet my needs, I'll do whatever I have to do to meet them myself—and it may be at your expense." She's developing a destructive mind-set that will cripple her ability to develop intimate relationships throughout life.

There is no more crucial lesson for growing up than learning to trust. An inability to trust impacts not only the child's horizontal relationships with other human beings, but their vertical relationship with God. It's difficult to learn to trust a loving Heavenly Father if you've experienced your earthly caregivers as being untrustworthy.

That's not to say all is lost if this first stage was deficient. There is always hope. God's grace covers a multitude of tough situations. But why not take the higher road and give your children the best possible impetus toward the next milestone.

Learning to Balance the Teetertotter (Early Childhood)

One small step for toddler, one giant step for the rest of the household! The day a child learns to walk, life is forever changed. A whole new world opens up to children as they make the amazing, liberating discovery that they have two legs that will carry them anywhere they want to go.

From the outset, let's declare the label "The Terrible Twos" taboo. This has become a popular description for this age-group that is reflective of parental frustration. Undeniably, developing an intimate relationship with a toddler can be trying. But this label implies that two-year-olds were somehow a mistake in God's plan. Imagine how one's perspective might be altered if we referred to this age as "The Terrific Twos." It really is, you know. Toddlers are accomplishing a very difficult, horizon-expanding task. They are learning how to balance autonomy and dependency. It might help to visualize this process if you conjured up a mental image of a teetertotter. On one side is *dependency* ("How long do I stay attached to Mommy and Daddy, depending on them for everything and doing everything they tell me to do?"). On the other side is *autonomy* ("I let go of Mommy and Daddy, do what I want, and begin to make my own decisions"). Achieving this balance is a lifelong endeavor, but it begins in earnest at this age.

Everything about this stage boils down to a process of *holding on* (dependency) and *letting go* (autonomy).

● Learning to walk — Pulling up on the coffee table, holding on for balance, and then letting go and taking off as fast and as far as little legs will cooperate

● Learning to talk — Holding on to their tongue muscles, their ideas, and the wind in their lungs — and then letting loose to the delight of adoring adults

● Potty training — You get the picture!

• Power struggles—Holding on and letting go of opinions and wills

A toddler's personality is characterized by holding on and letting go. One moment they're in Mommy's arms with a sweet, cherub-like smile, telling her with words and actions "I love you." Thirty seconds later they're down on the floor stomping their feet and saying, "No!" Holding on and letting go. Exasperating at times, but normal! That's not to say there's no place for limits at this age. Mom and Dad help balance this process by providing limits and controlling the consequences of the toddler's choices.

How can one help this holding on/letting go toddler navigate safe passage through this stage? First, teach them with words as well as actions about unconditional love. "I'm not going to let you run into the street. I'm not going to let you throw a ten-minute temper tantrum. By the same token, I'm not going to put you in a playpen with a box of animal crackers and expect you to be quiet all day. I am committed to do whatever is truly in your best interest." Avoid like the plague messages such as, "If you loved me, you'd take a nap like I asked you to." Or, "If you loved me, you wouldn't get mad when I have to tell you no." This is not an issue of love, unless the adults make it one. Unconditional love says not only do I love you, but because I love you I want to enter your toddler world and everything I say and do will truly be in your best interest, even when you don't understand it. And they won't. Count on it!

By the time this stage comes to a close, hopefully the toddler has resolved something called "splitting." Prior to this point, the toddler has seen Mommy and Daddy as having split personalities—Good Mommy/Bad Mommy and Good Daddy/Bad Daddy. Taking an "inside" look, it would go something like this. "Good Mommy brings me my blanket and gives me a snack. She loves me, and I love her. Bad Mommy makes me take a nap when I don't want to and won't let me have a cookie before dinner. She must not love me, and I don't love her. Good Daddy wrestles with me on the floor and reads me a story before bed. He loves me, and I love him. Bad Daddy tells me no when I try to get the goldfish out of its bowl and won't let me pull the dog's tail. He must not love me, and I don't love him."

If a child has seen unconditional love in action, by the end of toddlerhood she will have integrated the two mommies and two daddies and will begin to perceive that, "The mommy who feeds me, plays with me, cuddles me is the same mommy who sometimes tells me no and doesn't let me do what I want. She loves me, and I love her. The daddy who carries me on his shoulders and pulls me in my wagon is the same daddy who sometimes gets upset at what I've done and puts me in time-out. He loves me, and I love him. It's *because* they love me that they discipline me. Their rules protect me."

Resolution of this process of "splitting" is crucial for the healthy development of a child's concept of God. "The same God who loves me also disciplines me. He sees my mistakes and loves me anyway. Just because He does things that I don't like doesn't mean He doesn't love me. In fact, it's because He does."

Discovering a New World (Middle Childhood)

Many writers have described these as "The Magic Years." Having gained a pretty good handle (at least for now!) on balancing the teetertotter, they now begin the next exciting leg of their developmental journey. Although historians have ascribed the title of "Discoverer of the New World" to Christopher Columbus, let it be declared henceforth and forevermore that preschoolers are busy about this task every single day. Life is an adventure. Everything for them is new and exciting. Curiosity may have killed the cat, but it's the lifeblood of the preschooler. Each new discovery helps them define their identity in several key areas:

Physically

Kids this age are really into demonstrating how strong they are—flexing what they consider to be their Schwarzenegger-like muscles to convince any naysayers. They need a safe place to run, jump, and climb not only for the necessary physical exercise it affords their growing bodies but also because it allows them to make daily discoveries about who they are physically.

Part of this discovery process is their fascination with body parts. They begin to ask lots of questions. Much to the chagrin of red-faced parents, these questions are often blurted out in the most embarrassing places—and never in a whispered voice. The grocery store aisle or checkout line seems to lend itself readily to these exchanges. Although mortifying to parents, these questions are sincere and innocent—and deserve answers. Save the "Everything You Need to Know" version for later. Preschool 101 will suffice for now.

They're great imitators too. If you give a three- or four-year-old a football after they've watched a game on TV, they'll take it into the yard and run back and forth shouting orders to their imaginary teammates, convinced they're the world's greatest (strongest and fastest!) football player. They have no idea (and don't care) what the rules or objectives are.

This penchant for imitating behavior is one of the dangers of TV as they have no concept of the danger of much of what they're watching. Sammy ended up in the hospital after trying to leap off the roof. It looked so easy when Superman did it. Sammy couldn't understand why he ended up in an ambulance. That never happened to Superman.

Cognitively/Emotionally

Parents could retire by age forty if they had a dollar for every time their preschooler asks, "Why?"

"Why is the sky blue?"

"Because God made it that way."

"Why?"

"Why do I have to take a nap?"

"Because your body needs the rest."

"Why?"

"Why can't Daddy stay home today?"

"He has to go to work."

"Why?"

Although it can be grating on the nerves, this God-given curiosity and sense of "I wonder why" is a tool to help them learn how to cope with the world around them. Two-year-olds didn't worry about it; they coped by assuming they were the center of the universe. Three-year-olds make the discovery they're not and have to figure out where to go next. How do they do that? How do you help them?

You could try the lecture circuit. "Sit down. I need to tell you a few things in order for you to make your way in this world. First of all, you should never, ever steal things because it breaks statute 305.42 and a policeman might arrest you someday if you get caught." You could try this approach, but your success rate would be zilch. God didn't design kids this age to learn about the world around them simply through facts, lectures, and information. This is hard for a generation obsessed with the Information Super Highway to swallow! Facts play a part, but God has given us a greater opportunity to teach kids about their world through pursuing intimacy. What does this look like at this age?

God has gifted them to be able to learn about the world they live in through fantasy, through their imagination. They must be able to balance this fantasy and imagination with reality, but they can't do this alone. Guess who gets to help them with the balance? Mom, Dad, and other caring adults.

Every child this age must have times when they're in fantasy and times when they're in reality. Sometimes in our striving (albeit well-meaning striving!) to be perfect parents we tend to go to one of two extremes: On one end are parents who say, "I want my child to be creative, unstifled, uninhibited. I want him to be able to explore everything, do everything, fantasize about everything." They set no limits—ever. That approach will eventually drive you crazy!

On the other side, there are parents who say, "My kid is

going to live in the real world. Forget fantasy. Get real, kid! Straighten up. That fantasy stuff is a waste of time, and it's all of the devil anyway." This approach is equally unproductive. The goal is balance. Easier said than done, but here are some suggestions to get you started.

First, read to your child . . . read to your child . . . read to your child. God has enabled them to learn about the world through storytelling and imagination. Reading affords marvelous opportunities for teaching values as you capitalize on their development strengths. Sit down with them and read a story, be it a Bible story, a fairy tale, a favorite book. They'll soak it up, and you'll have a captive audience.

Second, play with your child . . . play with your child . . . play with your child. Playing is a lost art for most Americans. For a lot of reasons, we're all too busy with the "important" things in life to have time to play with our kids. Television is stealing this opportunity away from us not only because of the quantity of programming available but because it's such a readily accessible baby-sitter. Kids spend more time interacting with the tube than they do with their parents. Who do you want teaching your kids how to cope with the world?

And, as odd as this may sound, toys can destroy play. There are some incredible toys available to kids these days—if parents could just afford the batteries for them. But many of these toys are so elaborate that they do everything for the child, leaving nothing to the imagination. Parents, if we're honest, we often buy these toys for ourselves and then get our feelings hurt when our kids aren't interested in playing with them beyond Christmas morning. You can teach your child any lesson you want by getting down on their level and playing with them.

Sexually

Kids this age are also discovering who they are sexually. There are several key times in developing sexuality in a child, and this is one of them. Notice, we're using the term "sexuality" — not "sex." Sexuality is a child's sense of maleness or femaleness. They're discovering what it means to be a little girl or little boy.

Imagine, if you will, that you're a little boy about three and a half. You're going to begin to say things like,

"Mommy, I want to sit next to you in the car."

"Mommy, can we play a game together?"

"Daddy, get lost. I'm with Mommy now."

"I want Mommy to put me to bed."

"Mommy, I'm going to marry you."

Little boys want to attach to their mommies. It's normal. And dads hate it!

Paul threw his professional training out the window when it came to Matthew's desire to be with Vicky. Coming home after a long day of helping kids and their families learn how to relate better to one another, Paul was primed for his little boy to jump into his outstretched arms and tell him he was the world's best dad. Nothing doing. Matthew wanted to be with Mommy. Paul Warren, behavioral pediatrician, responded like any other normal dad — his feelings were hurt. "Vicky, can't you make him. . . . "

But toward the end of this stage something began to happen. This little guy began to notice that the strongest relationship in the family seemed to be between Mommy and Daddy. "Mommy loves me, but she and Daddy have something super special." So by the time he's four and a half or five his thinking begins to change. Now he says, "You know what? I want to be like my daddy. It's OK to be male. I want to grow up to be just like my daddy, and someday when I grow up I'll marry a lady just like my mommy." (Moms, this same process goes on between dads and daughters as well.)

Empathy

Empathy is the opposite of believing you're the center of the universe. It's the opposite of entitlement (the belief that "Everything should be the way I want it to be. Everyone else should agree with me"). Preschoolers begin to discover that somebody may feel something different than they do; somebody may actually have different thoughts and opinions than they do.

Begin to develop a "feeling vocabulary." Talk about feelings as you see sadness, anger, frustration, fear. Helping them learn to identify these feelings first in themselves will aid them in then recognizing them in others. Another avenue for modeling empathy is being willing to apologize and request forgiveness. As you attach value to their feelings and opinions by acknowledging when you have hurt them, it sets an example for them to follow.

Building Identities One Block at a Time (Late Childhood)

Psychiatrists used to call this stage "latency" because it was thought nothing much was happening or going on inside the child. What a misnomer! These kids are about the task of finding out more about themselves and establishing their identity as the child God has created them to be. They accomplish this through:

Sibling Rivalry

One of the most frequently asked questions when we conduct seminars is, "What can I do about sibling rivalry?" Our answer that kids need to have sibling rivalry in order to find out who they are is met with resounding groans and scattered boos and hisses. Fortunately for us, no tomatoes are allowed in the auditorium or a plummeting barrage would surely ensue. Considered by most parents to be a scourge from God meted out as punishment for past sins, sibling rivalry is actually an important and necessary "gift" to kids. Kids need sibling rivalry in order to find out who they are. They have to bounce off each other (sometimes literally!) to figure out their limits, their strengths and weaknesses, their uniqueness, and to develop problem-solving skills.

Normal sibling rivalry is not the evil nemesis we've made it out to be. However, sometimes sibling rivalry runs amuck when kids are getting seriously hurt physically and/or emotionally or when there are never any positive times. Lots of brothers and sisters who fight are also close and share good times together. When sibling rivalry falls into the "run amuck" category, it's usually not a sibling problem — it's a parent problem. In these instances, one or several of the following are usually going on. First, one or both of the parents consistently favor one of the kids. Emphasis here is on "consistently" because every day in your home there's probably one of your kids you don't like very much, who's on "your bad side." That's just part of growing up in a family. But when one or both parents consistently favor one of the children intense sibling rivalry will develop. Second, destructive sibling rivalry occurs when there are problems in the parents' marriage. Kids are incredible barometers of their parents' marriage, and when the marriage is consistently going downhill kids will start fighting. It's as though they're entreating their parents, "Whoa, Mom . . . Dad . . . Deflect a little of that tension and anger in our direction. Don't fight with each other . . . referee our fights instead." The third cause is when one of the parents, usually Dad, is too involved outside the home. In order to get Dad back home, the kids will act as ornery as they need to to get his attention and bring him back home. "Yoo-hoo . . . Dad . . . This calls for your touch. You're the only one who can handle us. Better come on home."

Competition

Adults who brag that their children's programs are competition-free are deluding themselves. Where there are kids, there's competition. Much like healthy sibling rivalry, healthy competition gives kids an opportunity to figure out their strengths and weaknesses, their boundaries, and how to solve problems. Healthy competition has three parameters:

The first is adult involvement. If you've ever spent time with a group of kids this age when they're out on the playground, you know that it takes about five minutes before somebody's complaining, "He cheated! It's not fair! You're stupid!" An adult needs to be available so these kids can ask for the adult's help to get things settled.

Second, every young person needs to have the opportunity to win in some endeavor. And every young person needs the opportunity to lose. That may sound heartless, but "healthy" competition affords both the opportunity to win and lose. What better time to learn how to handle defeat than while under the protective umbrella of a loving, supportive home environment.

Another integral piece to the identity puzzle is having the experience of being part of a team. This is of particular importance in this "Me" generation that says that the most important things in life are personal freedom and self-sufficiency. "I don't need anybody. I can pull myself up. I don't need any help." That's not biblical. The Bible emphasizes loving one another, serving one another, working together, living together. A team experience whether it's sports, Scouts, church groups, or other civic groups gives kids the opportunity to experience interdependency and support.

Fairness

By this time, parents have heard the complaint "It's not fair!" ad nauseam. Our standard reply? "Whoever said life was fair? Why, when I was your age . . . " This reply tastes satisfying as it rolls off the tongue but evaporates immediately upon hitting the air. It does nothing to build the relationship. OK, life isn't fair. So now what? What do you hold on to?

Trying to base your family on fairness—at least the way grade-schoolers measure it (in microns!)—is impossible. If things were *fair*, the chocolate cake would have to be divided exactly, not one crumb more or less. In order to be *fair*, your nine-year-old would have to go to bed at the same time as your one-year-old. After all, that's the only *fair* way. But then, of course, a cry of "But that's not fair!" would fill the room. And round and round you'd go.

Arguing and trying to explain why your way really is fair is as ineffective and as painful as beating your head against a brick wall. The higher road takes the approach that says, "This is not an issue of fairness. It's an issue of trust. I know it doesn't seem fair, and I understand you're upset. But trust me; this is the way it needs to be."

Achievement

Kids this age must experience the success of achievement in three ways. First, they must see themselves as successful in the eyes of their parents in some endeavor. A word of caution here. This does not mean that their worth is based in what they do. This is a delicate balance, as precarious as walking a tightrope. This may be more challenging for some parents. If your child isn't a great student, is a klutz on the ball field, can't draw, can't sing, can't play an instrument, and isn't the cutest kid in school, you're going to have to dig a little deeper. But keep digging! Keep in mind, this pursuit is not so you can look good through your child, but so she can experience a sense of affirmation and approval from you.

Second, they must see themselves as successful in the eyes of their peers. Case in point: Remember those horrible rainy days you used to dread back in grade school? You couldn't go out at recess so they'd take you to this dark, dingy room they called a gym. The teacher, desperate for a break, would just leave you in the room with these parting instructions (which fell with the weight of a death sentence on some shoulders), "OK, you guys play basketball. Johnny and Susie, you two will be the captains. Choose your teams, and I'll see you in about fifteen minutes." And so the agony begins. The really cool kids are drafted first; the mediocre kids go in the second round. Then the two captains hem and haw around for what seems like an eternity because they don't really want any of the remaining reluctant recruits. Or, there's the pain of being the one who never got an invitation to the birthday party of the century. Peer rejection cuts deeply, and the wounds heal slowly. One proactive parental step in this regard can be cultivating family friends with positive peer influences. Don't leave your child to travel this peer journey alone—get involved.

Third, every grade-schooler must see themselves as successful in the eyes of adults other than their parents. Think back to your grade school years. Who was your significant other adult? Was it a teacher? A coach? A Scout master? A Sunday School teacher? A favorite aunt or uncle? Whoever it was, their supportive encouragement spurred you on to take a few risks and reach for stars that you might otherwise have viewed as unattainable. They played a pivotal role in shaping your sense of identity.

These building blocks now seemingly in place, everything's about to come tumbling down when our grade-schooler hits fifth grade.

Change, Change, Change! (Adolescence)

Stepping Away (Early Adolescence)

Early adolescence begins in about fifth grade and continues through the junior high years. Some incredibly exciting things are happening for these kids as they cease being little boys and little girls and become young men and women. In fact, fifth grade is perhaps the most important of all twelve grades. The research tells us, and clinical experience bears it out, that people who have serious psychological difficulties later in life (in their thirties and forties) made their decision about the worthwhileness of life most often somewhere in fifth grade. These kids desperately need parents and other adults who will enter their world and walk through this time with them.

Most people think this is the age when puberty (what an ugly word!) begins, but it actually begins at age five or six with gradual, ever-so-minimal hormonal changes. Quick, grab the smelling salts. Mom just fainted! But a massive explosion occurs around fifth grade. Girls take the lead, usually beginning at about nine and a half or ten. They experience their growth spurt early in puberty and then begin their periods toward the end. Boys begin puberty later, around age ten and a half to eleven, and are the exact opposite. Their sex hormones begin to flow in early puberty, and their growth spurt kicks in almost at the end (much to their chagrin!).

The interesting thing about sexuality in early adolescents is that at no other time is maleness and femaleness more different than in junior high. Boys are incredibly physical. They're curious about what things look like, what they feel like. Romance? Forget it! Girls are all romance. Knights on white horses. "Ooooh. He may call me tonight. He's soooo dreamy." Physical? Forget it! And so, wherever you have hordes of junior high boys and girls together, you'll find the boys whispering and chuckling, chasing and teasing the girls, looking for opportunities to touch them, pinch them, pull their bra straps. While the girls are screaming, "Stop it! Stop it!" But underneath they're cooing, "I love it. Maybe he'll call me tonight and we'll fall in love."

Two messages for parents here. One is to understand that this is normal. You can't get to healthy adulthood without going through these junior high years. Do you want them acting like they're in junior high now . . . or when they're thirty? Take your choice. Second, there's a strong message here regarding dating. Kids this age going on one-on-one dates is a disaster waiting to happen. Their interests are so totally divergent—boys all physical/girls all romance—that they'll be horribly uncomfortable. They're thinking, "Is this all there is to a relationship? No thanks."

Their thoughts and feelings are undergoing some major transformations as well. Several things begin to happen. First, they have an attack of aphasia. This is a fancy medical term meaning they don't talk . . . at least not to parents. So, you have these kinds of conversations.

"What did you do in school today?"

"Nothin'."

"What did you have for lunch?"

"Don't remember."

"What would you like to do tonight?"

"I don't know."

This is exasperating to parents because the perception is that they're intentionally withholding information just to be irritating. Actually, their thoughts and feelings are so new and so overwhelming that they couldn't find words to express them even if they understood them—which they don't!

They're also incredibly disorganized. If you need proof, go to any junior high or middle school and look inside some of their lockers. Or, look in their notebooks and you'll find papers stashed every which way. Math papers in the English folder; love notes in the science folder, a three-month-old permission slip that never made it home. Contrary to the opinion of the adults in their lives, their disorganization doesn't stem from laziness or willful carelessness. Life is suddenly so incredibly different and overwhelming they just can't keep up the pace. It's amazing how many kids who were previously well-organized and successful students now hit fifth and sixth grade and are out-to-lunch. What do they need from adults? They don't need to be put down or shot out of the saddle. "What's wrong with you? Are you ever going to get yourself organized?" That just reinforces exactly what they're thinking about themselves. "I may never get organized. I may never get out of this." They need empathy and structure.

These kids are also experiencing ambivalence for the first time. Ambivalence looks something like this: "The same people that I really love also make me so mad sometimes that I feel like I hate them." They discover that the things in life that are really scary are also pretty exciting. For months before starting junior high or middle school they hear the horror stories about kids getting lost and how kids in the hall appear from nowhere and beat you up and try to flush your head down the toilet. On the one hand, they're scared to death. On the other, they can't wait. They can't imagine anything more exciting.

Separation and individuation becomes a major issue. Big

words that simply mean moving away from your parents and becoming the person God has created you to be. Hopefully, this process has been taking place in small increments from day one, but it bursts onto the scene full steam ahead at this age. Wish we could tell you it will be resolved by eighth grade—No can do! (For some it's not resolved until thirty-five . . . thirty-nine . . . forty-three. . . !)

At the same time this is going on, these kids are also making the horrifying discovery that the parents they've depended on for everything for so long are, after all, imperfect. The same parents who were once thought to have all the answers, now seem to know nothing. How can this be? It must be that these are not the real parents. There must be perfect parents out there somewhere. Many kids who are not adopted begin to wonder if they really were adopted, that somehow they were switched in the nursery, and that their real parents are out there somewhere. Adopted kids are convinced that their biological parents are the perfect parents and long to locate them. Children of divorce assume that the parent who doesn't live with them is the perfect parent.

Sadly, at a time when kids need adults the most, this is the age that adults avoid like the plague. In most churches, you find adults who love working with the high schoolers and who gravitate to the younger kids because they're cute and fun. But when it comes to junior high kids, "I served my time." What an opportunity awaits adults who are willing to roll up their sleeves and get involved. These kids don't need head-wagging naysayers. They need adults who are available to provide empathy, understanding, and structure.

Bold New Steps (Middle Adolescence)

Having survived junior high with a scrapbook full of memories that might best be described as "The Agony and the Ecstasy II," our heroes now embark on the second leg of their adolescent journey somewhere around fourteen. They'll be on this road for about three years.

Whereas they have previously depended on their peer group *as a group*, they're now capable of some one-on-one relationships. Their commitment to those relationships, however, vacillates from day to day. One day they're best friends. They're going to grow up together, go to college together, go into business together. Best friends forever. Inseparable. Two weeks later, "I can't stand that person. I don't ever want to see her again." Two weeks later . . . fused at the hip again. Up and down. It's a normal part of growing up, but they need adults in their life to help establish healthy boundaries and appropriate expectations.

They are also actively resolving the issue of *egocentricity* (self-centeredness). The first way this manifests itself is that they make the assumption that the world is their stage and they're performing for an adoring audience. If you've ever been to DisneyWorld during the summer, you've undoubtedly seen groups of kids this age climbing the rails, screaming and yelling at people 500 yards away, assuming everybody wants to know they're there. Paradoxically, at this age something we affectionately refer to as "the zit principle" kicks in. That is, they assume that all people see are their negative characteristics.

Debbie was a straight-A student, until she was required to take a speech class and received a resounding F. She steadfastly refused to get up and give a speech simply because there was a small zit on the tip of her nose. Although it was so microscopic one would have to strain to see it from a foot away, she was convinced that all eyes would be riveted on her zit, that she would be the class joke and would be humiliated beyond recovery.

Adolescents' egocentricity is also evident in their powerful feeling of uniqueness. This comes out in two ways. One is they know everything, and parents know nothing. But, while they know lots of facts and understand the tragic consequences of such activities as drugs, premarital sex, smoking, and drinking, their sense of uniqueness translates into a belief that those things only happen to other people, not to them. They also assume that because their thoughts and feelings are so new to them that they must be new to every one else as well. So conversations similar to this one begin to occur. Your sixteen-year-old daughter retorts, "But, Mom, you just don't understand. You've never been in love before." And she actually believes it.

Incredibly idealistic, they go for the highest goods . . . but they're also enticed by the highest of the highs and the lowest of the lows. That's one reason why rock music can be dangerous. Drugs, obviously, are dangerous because they feed off this love of experiencing new ranges of feelings. As Christian parents, we must be careful not to present a relationship with Jesus Christ only as "getting high on Jesus." That will appeal to them at this developmental phase, but what happens when they reach a low point in their life? If they associate Jesus Christ only with the "highs," they will begin to flounder in their faith. They need a more complete picture, a firmer foundation upon which to build.

Sexuality, much like their hormonal curve, could be graphically depicted by a roller coaster . . . ups and downs . . . incredibly high/latent, incredibly high/latent. Consequently, these kids do not belong on one-on-one car dates with nothing to do. Leaving home with the best of intentions, their hormone curve kicks into high gear and you suddenly have two teenagers in a car with time on their hands and nothing to do. In other words, you have trouble.

These kids don't need adults in their lives who think their generation has gone to the dogs. They need adults who remember what it was like to be a teenager. Like their predecessors, they need lots of understanding and empathy. Redeem the time. Their years at home are rapidly coming to an end.

The Final Leg (Late Adolescence)

The final leg of the adolescent journey begins at around age seventeen and ends by twenty-one . . . twenty-five . . . thirty . . . forty. . . . They are now ready for relationships that are characterized not by the up and down curve but by intimacy. Not sexual intimacy, not marriage . . . but a decision to have relationships characterized by a commitment to the other person and the other person's best interests rather than on self-gratification.

This is the ultimate goal they began targeting back in their toddler days—balancing the teetertotter of autonomy and dependency. They've now hopefully achieved *autonomy with attachment.* "I will be responsible for myself. I'm not going to ask or expect someone else to be responsible for my feelings and my behavior" *(autonomy).* "But I realize I can't, and don't want to be, a lone ranger. I'll also be committed to caring involvement with other people and relationships" *(attachment).*

By the time adolescence is over, they will have finally resolved the storm that began when they were eleven or twelve and discovered their parents were not perfect. Adolescence is not truly over until this issue is successfully resolved. People fall into three different camps in their attempts to do this.

First is the group who continue to rage against their parents. "I can't believe the mistakes my parents made. I'm never going to get over this. They really messed up and messed me up in the process. I'm so mad at them."

The second group takes a totally opposite stance. "My parents were the most perfect parents who ever lived on the face of the earth. They never made any mistakes." Impossible! Imperfect people are destined to make mistakes.

Then there's the group in the middle. "Yes, my parents were not perfect. I wish my dad had not done some of the things he did. And I wish my mom had done more of this. But, you know what, I've worked through that and have forgiven them, come to love them more, and I'm now ready to move on with my life. God expects me to be responsible for being a good steward of the life He's given me."

The first group puts their parents on trial, so to speak, and never lets them off the witness stand. In their self-appointed position of raging prosecutor, they allow no opportunity for forgiveness. The second group goes to the opposite extreme. They choose instead to deny the truth, assuming that this is how they obey the biblical command to "honor your father and mother." The group in the middle offer and find forgiveness through the direction of their Heavenly Father. "My mom and dad made mistakes. They were imperfect parents, just as I'm imperfect." They've discovered that truly honoring your father and mother means being committed to the truth. Only then can one truly finish growing up. "You shall know the truth, and the truth shall make you free" (John 8:32).

God has a beautiful plan for growing up. Take time to appreciate it. Allow your kids to enjoy each day and to feel your approval for who they are right now.

Walk . . . Don't Run. Every Day Is Important!

Ask Yourself

1. Take time to review the developmental stage for each of your children. According to this chapter, what developmental tasks lay before them? Put yourself in their shoes; focus on their perspective; enter their world for a few moments. Now determine your child's greatest needs and ways you might meet them. Be specific.

2. Psalm 139 tells us that we are "fearfully and wonderfully made." God has made each of us uniquely different. Think about the way God has designed your child. What temperament characteristics (adaptability, rhythmicity, energy level, etc.) are present? How are these the same or different from you? Your spouse? Other siblings? What challenges have resulted? Are any of these challenges present because of an attempt to change God-given characteristics? Be especially alert to any statements of comparison that may be a subtle attempt to change a child. Statements like, *Why can't you be more like . . .* communicate a lack of acceptance.

Experiencing Truth

According to Psalm 127, our children are God's gifts to us. You might want to write a thank-You note this week. Tell

God about your appreciation for the child He's given you. Mention the specific things you like about "the gift." What character traits do you find most precious? Let God know of your gratefulness for such a priceless gift. After the thank-You note is written, you will want to think of ways to communicate these same thoughts to your child. Mail a card, give a hug, then verbalize to your child your gratefulness. You might want to give him a copy of your letter to God.

Special Thoughts for Single Parents

After determining your child's developmental stage, identify her outstanding emotional need(s). Make a simple plan to meet these needs. Focus on what you can do and then involve other adults if needed. For example, you may not be able to build Lego castles with your five-year-old every day, but you can give attention by reading bedtime stories. Your adolescent will appreciate your support when you take fifteen minutes to call her after school—just to see how her friends responded to her new glasses.

Some of these needs may be difficult for you to meet yourself—such as male companionship (attention/training), or female companionship (nurturing/comfort). Become proactive. Expand your "family of choice" to include other adults who might meet these needs. You might establish relationships with church groups, community groups, or partnerships with intact families.

Special Thoughts for Blended Families

The response to divorce and remarriage will be different according to a child's age and development. Children may be very expressive about their loss, verbalizing their unsettled or hostile feelings. Their grief may also reveal itself in more subtle ways. They may show signs of regression—bedwetting or thumbsucking—or display poor performance in school. Teens are most likely to demonstrate their grief through acting-out behaviors.

Consider how each of your children responds to the divorce and remarriage. How has each child dealt with his loss? Have you disciplined acting-out behavior but still maintained an atmosphere of openness? Have you provided opportunities for each child to share his concerns about the absent parent? The new living arrangements? The new stepparent? The new siblings? Tell each child you want to hear concerns and then make time to do so.

CHAPTER 3

A Home Environment for Intimacy...Liberty or Bondage?

WHEW! THROUGH THE wonders of modern time travel, you've just covered nineteen years in the space of one chapter. It's reminiscent of one of those workaholic-designed vacation packages where you visit five national parks in four days. Exhausting!

Much has been written in recent years about the short- and long-term effects of stress in the workplace. High blood pressure, fatigue, anxiety, heart problems, sleep problems, and digestive disorders are just a few of the ailments that have been linked to stress overload. Studies have been conducted and strategies implemented for providing a more stress-free environment in order to improve work conditions and, thereby, increase productivity.

Ever thought about the stress level in your child's work environment? To do so would first require answering the question, "What is the work of childhood?" Going to school? Doing homework? Taking out the trash and making their beds? Making sure they never drip ketchup on their shirts or belch in public? Going to church every Sunday? Making his parents look good? Sorry! All those things may be taking place, but the work of childhood is two simple but insightful words—two words, whose reality is elusive but to experience them is liberating. The two words? Succinctly put, the job of a child is to *grow up!* He may go out into the world laboratory for periods of time to execute responsibilities such as school, play, etc., but the real "work" is accomplished at home. The environment that greets him and sustains him will have a tremendous impact on whether he flourishes or flounders.

Home: A Place of Liberty or Bondage?

As they're growing up, children are rapidly building their "belief system" about themselves and about life. They are "tape-recording" and storing in their cognitive computer banks important parental messages received verbally and nonverbally. Both positive and negative messages are cataloged as if they were true—whether they are or not. Whether intentionally conveyed or not, their impact is felt just the same. While few parents would intentionally convey unhealthy belief systems to their children, we sometimes fall prey to "worldly wisdom" and foist it upon our children without realizing its venomous nature.

The following tidbit of information will come as no great revelation but provides a prime example of this unhealthy way of thinking that impacts us all. We live in a world that operates on the premise of "doing" things in order to be "OK." We work to keep jobs and work even harder to get raises. Performance = Worthiness. The emphasis is on what we *"do"* not on who we *"are."* God has a different set of criteria. Working hard can't make us "OK" with Him. "He saved us, not on the basis of deeds which we have done in righteousness, but according to His mercy, by the washing of regeneration and renewing by the Holy Spirit" (Titus 3:5).

If, as we established in chapter 1, each of us is born with needs for acceptance, approval, and comfort, what must we "do" in order to receive them? Must they be earned through *acceptable performance* or can they be *freely received?* This probing question begs for an honest answer because these two paths are diametrically opposed to one another. One leads to bondage; the other to liberty. Satan would like nothing better than for every human being on Planet Earth to be in bondage, but it was for freedom that Christ died. Jesus said we are to be in the world but not of the world. Choose to take the path that leads to liberty. Here are some road markers that will guide your way:

"Be" then "Do"

It's essential to keep the correct order. Intimate relationships are founded upon first *"being"* accepted, loved, and
valued . . . a desire to *"do"* things consistent with this acceptance, love, and worth then follows. Why should one for
whom Christ freely died have to earn my acceptance?
What gives me the right to withhold that which I freely
received in Christ? What did I (or you) do to receive . . .

Love

"And walk in love, just as Christ also loved you, and
gave Himself up for us, an offering and a sacrifice to
God as a fragrant aroma" (Eph. 5:2).

Acceptance

"Wherefore, accept one another, just as Christ also accepted us to the glory of God" (Rom. 15:7).

Kindness/Forgiveness

"Let all bitterness and wrath and anger and clamor and
slander be put away from you, along with all malice.
And be kind to one another, tender-hearted, forgiving
each other, just as God in Christ also has forgiven you"
(Eph. 4:31-32).

Comfort

"Who comforts us in all our affliction so that we may be
able to comfort those who are in any affliction with the
comfort with which we ourselves are comforted by God"
(2 Cor. 1:4).

The answer is blatantly obvious—We did NOTHING to
deserve these things. Christ set the precedent. He established
the pattern. He gave freely; we received. Therefore, as we
have freely received, we are to freely give (Matt. 10:8).

Trying to live on the world's performance treadmill leads to nowhere and hinders relationships in the process. The broad path of performance is one that many families travel, but its end is destructive. The narrow path of unconditional giving is one that few families travel, but its end is greatly blessed.

Gratefulness Motivates

Every parent longs for—prays for—obedient children. Certainly nothing wrong with that! Part of the job of parenting is to raise responsible children who are obedient to parents, appropriate authority figures and, of course, to God. But it's not sufficient to look at a child's positive behaviors and pat yourself on the back and congratulate yourself on a job well done. The job's not done until you've looked beneath the surface to see what's motivating the behaviors, and that's often the hardest part.

Imagine we've employed a video surveillance camera to document the comings and goings of Timothy and Daniel for a month. At the end of that time, we watch the film and see exactly the same thing. Both boys are obedient, polite, dutiful young men. But the word "video" itself implies the weakness in our methodology. All we have is what we can *see*. We know nothing about what's going on beneath the surface.

Timothy's obedience is motivated by fear: fear that he could lose the love of his parents if he doesn't perform according to their expectations, fear of failure, fear that his needs won't be met if he doesn't do everything perfectly. Performing out of obligation is impossible to sustain over the long haul. "Doing" things in order to gain the approval, acceptance, and love of others becomes a hollow victory. What happens when Timothy goes to college and that fear of parental disapproval is no longer as pervasive? Behavior that looked good on the surface turns to irresponsibility and hinders him from reaching his God-given potential.

Daniel's obedience is motivated by gratefulness for having already received approval, acceptance, and love from his parents and from God. Knowing that his parents consider him a valuable "gift" from the Lord, he is likewise motivated to be a wise steward of his God-given talents and abilities.

Be careful not to put too much emphasis on how things look. This is a temptation for all of us because we want others to think we're doing a good job as parents. Keep in mind that the central issues are issues of the heart. Man looks at the outward appearance; God looks at the heart (1 Sam. 16:7).

As always when we look for a perfect example, we look to the life of Jesus Himself. In the Gospel accounts of Jesus' first day of public ministry we find Him going down to the River Jordan to submit Himself to John to be baptized. First, He hears the testimony of John—"Behold, the Lamb of God who takes away the sin of the world!" and then comes confirmation of even greater significance. When He comes up out of the water, the heavens open, the Spirit of God descends on Him like a dove, and a voice speaks. "You are My beloved Son in whom I am well pleased." Let's stop right there. You miss the whole import of this passage if you think that was said for the crowd's benefit. That was the Heavenly Father affirming His Child. "You are My beloved Son in whom I am well pleased." The beautiful part of this story is that Jesus hadn't yet preached a sermon or performed a miracle. And yet His Father affirmed Him. He blessed Him because of who He was, not what He'd done.

Scripture tells us that immediately thereafter Jesus spent forty days and forty nights in the wilderness where He was tempted by the devil. Can you imagine how His Father's blessing must have sustained Him! Could it be that part of what prompted, undergirded, and motivated the earthly ministry of Jesus was an overwhelming sense of gratefulness for that blessing? As He ministered during the ensuing three years of His life, He was intimately acquainted with sorrow and grief but always had those words locked in His heart and ringing in His ears—"This is My beloved Son in whom I am well pleased."

Go ye and do likewise . . . Try this homework assignment.

Sometime today when one of your children walks by you, interject yourself into the life of that child unexpectedly and say something like this, "You know, I was reminded again today how much I love you and how proud I am to have you as my son (or daughter)." Then just hug him and walk on. Just leave him standing there in the awe and wonder of "What did I do to deserve that?" He has to end up with the conclusion—Nothing! In other words, live out and "experience" this passage of Scripture. It will produce an empowering sense of gratefulness in your children.

Grace Liberates

Christmas 1991 brought a buzz of excitement to the Warren household. Matthew was anticipating Christmas morning with the enthusiasm and curiosity typical of a seven-year-old boy with visions of Nintendo dancing in his head. Adding to the holiday hypermania was the fact that Paul's parents were visiting. One afternoon as Vicky wrapped the last of the gifts and placed it strategically under the tree, Matthew made an announcement.

"Mommy, I have a great idea about how we can pass out the presents Christmas morning."

In her mind she entertained the slightly cynical thought, "Would it happen to include starting with you first?"

But, God graciously kept the words deep in her throat; and she responded in a kinder manner. "And what would that be, Sweetie?"

"Well, I think we should go from oldest to youngest. So we would start with Granddaddy, then Grandmother, then Daddy, then you, and then me."

Taking into account the Warren tradition of opening presents, this was quite a suggestion. As presents are passed out, each person opens one gift while the others watch. It can be quite time consuming, especially for a seven-year-old! There was no question Matthew was chomping at the bit to unwrap the mysteries that awaited him beneath the tree, as evidenced by the frequent shaking and rearranging of gifts that went on from morning to night.

What, then, would prompt such a generous gesture? Could it be that because his needs had been met, he felt no sense of urgency to "take" but could enjoy "giving" to others?

"It was for freedom that Christ set us free" (Gal. 5:1). Unconditionally loving a child "frees" her from performing in order to please people. Having truly partaken of grace, she is genuinely free to give to others. Having received that which she could not earn and did not deserve (i.e., grace), she is therefore free from fear of never having it and the fear of ever losing it. "Where the Spirit of the Lord is, there is liberty" (2 Cor. 3:17).

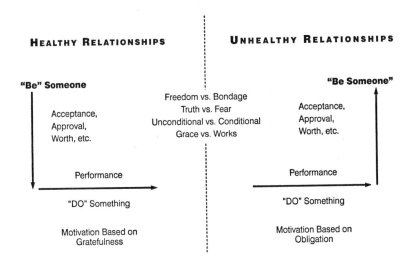

Communicating Appreciation

Having established that intimate relationships are possible when we accept one another for who we are rather than what we do, it's important then to communicate our appreciation for a person's character as well as his behavior.

The results are powerful. Expressing appreciation—particularly for character strengths—affirms a person's divinely declared worth and encourages him living in a manner "worthy of the calling" (Eph. 4:1).

Familiarize yourself with the following list of character qualities and look for opportunities to affirm and encourage your children. Try verbal affirmations, notes in their school lunches, notes on the refrigerator door, or if you're away record a message on the answering machine.

Alertness

Learning to pay attention to all the lessons God is teaching through authorities, friends, and experiences

Attentiveness

Learning who to be attentive to, what to listen for, and who not to listen to

Availability

Learning to reject distractions that hinder me from fulfilling my responsibilities

Boldness

Demonstrating the confidence that following the principles of Scripture will bring ultimate victory regardless of present opposition

Cautiousness

Gaining adequate counsel before making decisions. Recognizing temptations and fleeing them

Contentment

Learning to enjoy present possessions rather than desiring new or additional ones

Creativity

Finding ways to overcome seemingly impossible obstacles; discovering practical applications for spiritual principles

Decisiveness

Learning to finalize difficult decisions on the basis of God's ways, Word, and will

Deference

Limiting my freedom in order not to offend the personal preferences of those God has called me to serve

Dependability

Learning to be true to your word even when it is difficult to carry out what you promised to do

Determination

Learning to give whatever energy is necessary to complete a project

Diligence

Seeing every task as an assignment from the Lord and applying energy and concentration to accomplish it

Discernment

Knowing what to look for in evaluating people, problems, and things

Discretion

Knowing what is appropriate and what is inappropriate. Seeing the consequences of words and actions down the road

Endurance

Maintaining commitment to a goal during times of pressure. Recognizing and laying aside hindrances

Enthusiasm

Learning what actions and attitudes please God and becoming excited about them

Fairness

Looking at a situation through the eyes of each one involved in it

Faith

Developing an unshakable confidence in God and His Word. Identifying God's will and acting upon it

Flexibility

Learning how to cheerfully change plans when unexpected conditions require it

Forgiveness

Learning to demonstrate Christ's love toward others, remembering how much God has forgiven us

Generosity

Recognizing that all possessions belong to God. Learning how to be a wise steward of time, money, and possessions

Gentleness

Learning to respond to needs with kindness and love. Knowing what is appropriate for the emotional needs of others

Gratefulness

Learning to recognize the benefits which God and others have provided; looking for appropriate ways to express genuine appreciation

Hospitality

Learning how to provide an atmosphere which contributes to the physical and spiritual growth of those around us

Initiative

Taking steps to seek after God with our whole heart. Assuming responsibility for the physical, emotional, and spiritual encouragement of those around us

Joyfulness

Learning to be happy regardless of our outside circumstances

Love

Learning how to give to the basic needs of others without motive of personal reward; an unconditional commitment to an imperfect person

Loyalty

Adopting as your own the wishes and goals of those you are serving

Meekness

Learning how to yield rights and possessions to God. Learning to earn the right to be heard rather than demanding a hearing

Neatness

Learning to organize and care for personal possessions

Obedience

Yielding the right to have the final decision

Patience

Learning to accept difficult situations as from God without giving Him a deadline to remove the problem

Persuasiveness

Effectively presenting our case while demonstrating commitment to our convictions by the example of our lives

Punctuality

Showing esteem for other people and their time by not keeping them waiting

Resourcefulness

Seeing value in that which others overlook. Learning to make wise use of things which others would discard

Responsibility

Learning to establish personal restrictions and guidelines that are necessary to fulfill what you know you should do

Reverence

Learning to respect the authority and position of God to others

Security

Learning to exhibit a freedom from fear

Self-control

Learning to quickly identify and obey the initial promptings of the Holy Spirit. Bringing my thoughts, words, and actions under the control of the Holy Spirit

Sensitivity

Being alert to the promptings of the Holy Spirit. Avoiding danger by sensing wrong motives in others. Knowing how to give the right words at the right time

Sincerity

Having motives that are transparent. Having a genuine concern to benefit the lives of others

Thoroughness

Learning what details are important for the success of a project

Thriftiness

Knowing how to accomplish the most with the what's available

Tolerance

Learning how to respond to the immaturity of others without accepting their standard of immaturity

Truthfulness

Learning to share that which is right without misrepresenting the facts. Facing the consequences of a mistake

Understanding

Viewing life from another's perspective; looking past life's obvious disappointments to find the comfort of God

Virtue

Learning to build personal moral standards which will cause others to desire a more godly life

Wisdom

Learning to see life from God's perspective. Learning how to apply principles of life in daily situations

Discovering and expressing appreciation for your children's character traits communicates a genuine desire to know them intimately—inside out. As they sense that desire on your part, they will feel a greater freedom to come to you with the hurts and disappointments they will inevitably experience.

How Approachable Are You?

If home is to be a place of liberty where grace is spoken, parents must demonstrate a willingness to be vulnerable and approachable. Do your children have the liberty to share with you when they feel hurt by you? Misunderstood? Dealt with unfairly? Would you respond defensively or in anger if your child pointed out a perceived inconsistency?

Since repetition aids learning, let's reiterate what we established in a previous chapter: There are no perfect parents. Period. Because all parents are imperfect human beings, we all make mistakes, have weaknesses, and display inconsistencies. The crucial issue is whether we try to perpetuate the lie of infallibility or are openly vulnerable. Do we hypocritically wear the mask of perfection or display our approachability?

Healthy families deal with the reality of inevitable hurt. One of the most powerful ways to deal with the hurts that occur within the family is through confession and forgiveness. How long has it been since your children heard you genuinely apologize for some wrong on your part as a parent? If you are aware of ways you have hurt your spouse or children, take the initiative to confess to God and then to your family members. Hearing, "I was wrong, will you forgive me?" sends a powerful message to a child. It communicates a sense of value as well as gives them permission to make mistakes. "If Mom and Dad can admit mistakes, that must mean I can admit my mistakes. And if Mom and Dad can be forgiven for their mistakes—so can I. What a relief!"

There will be other times when your child will experience disappointments, hurts, losses, or misunderstandings and you'll be unaware of it. What do you do about those? Do your children feel the freedom to approach you with their hurts? Providing an atmosphere of approachability that offers comfort, not lectures or blame, will cultivate closeness and intimacy.

Why not set your sights on a new goal—establishing a heritage of sharing your life with your children through approachability. Dream of your children saying, "I know my parents loved me . . . "

- through the undivided attention they gave me.
- through their patient listening to my hurts and fears.
- through their empathy and openness as we shared feelings.
- through their valuing my thoughts and opinions.
- through their trust of my decisions and plans.
- through the common interests and fun we shared.
- through their verbalized appreciation and love.
- through their openness to touch, hug, and reassure me just with their presence.

Stimulate One Another to Love and Good Deeds

Some final thoughts from the Book of Hebrews. Although not intended as an exhortation specifically to parents, this challenge offers some valuable insights that parents would do well to implement—*"and let us consider how to stimulate one another to love and good deeds, not forsaking our own assembling together, as is the habit of some, but encouraging one another, and all the more, as you see the day drawing near"* (10:24-25).

Let us consider ...

Take a proactive stance rather than a reactive stance to parenting. The word "consider" implies pondering, thinking about, weighing the advantages and disadvantages of a decision, entering your child's world in order to assess her need.

how to stimulate ...

Your goal is to move them toward growth, to prompt them to action, to excite them about discovering who God has created them to be.

one another ...

Parenting with intimacy requires leaving the Lone Ranger lifestyle in the dust and riding the trail with the "pardners" God's entrusted to you.

to love and good deeds ...

With the right kind of root stimulators, positive emotions and behavior will grow in fertile soil and will result in an attitude of gratitude as they try their wings and begin to fly.

not forsaking our own assembling together as is the habit of some ...

Has "family time" been relegated to a back burner in order to make time for the myriad of activities that crowd out time for meaningful relationship-building?

but encouraging one another ...

Determine to make meeting one another's intimacy needs a priority. As you each step out the front door to face the world, what a fabulous feeling to know that you have a cheering section pulling for you!

and all the more as you see the day drawing near...

Children are bombarded with daily reminders that the world is an unsafe place. They see the faces of abducted children on milk cartons and grocery bags. As they flip through the newspaper on their way to the "funny papers" they pass story after story recounting incidents of kids killing kids and adults abusing kids that are sober reminders that the world in which they live is far from "funny." Radio, television, and movies add their gruesome contributions as well.

The challenge is great—raising confident, secure children in the middle of a world that is increasingly hostile toward them. But the promises of God's Word provide solace and encouragement. Clasp onto this one and hold on tight, "greater is He who is in you, than he who is in the world" (1 John 4:4).

As you therefore have received Christ Jesus the Lord,
so walk in Him, having been firmly rooted and now being
built up in Him and established in your faith, just as you
were instructed, and overflowing with gratitude.
Colossians 2:6-7

Ask Yourself

1. Which path are you currently traveling—the path that leads to bondage or the path that leads to liberty? Where has it taken you and your family?

2. Consider the overall environment of your home. Is it characterized by harmony or strife? Do family members feel secure or threatened? Do your children feel comfortable inviting friends over to visit? Are feelings of tension the exception or the rule?

Experiencing Truth

1. Practice the truth of John 17. Adopt an attitude at home that reflects "in the world but not of the world." Affirm your

children for just being your children. If you typically give incentives for grades or chores, give the same reward just because you love them. They'll wonder what the surprise is all about. Be sure to give a sincere reminder of your unconditional love. Give hugs for no apparent reason. Praise the efforts of a child — don't just comment on success or failure. Create a home environment that is characterized by grace, not by works. Begin parenting by grace.

2. First Thessalonians 5:11 says to "Encourage one another, and build up one another." Assign each family member a day of the week. On the assigned day, every other family member tells that person special qualities they appreciate about her. You may want to post the character qualities somewhere in the house where everyone can see them. Affirm personhood, not performance.

Special Thoughts for Single Parents

1. Loving children for who they are means communicating that love appropriately. Be careful of the traps that come with material possessions. Avoid the power struggle of competing with another parent or family in giving money or gifts. Avoid trying to buy your way into your child's life. Seize the moments available to give what money can't buy. Meeting emotional needs is more important than financial status.

2. Prepare to answer the tough questions, if you haven't already. Show your commitment to acceptance by helping your child understand the divorce and cope with the results. Be sure your child knows the divorce was in no way his or her fault. Affirm them for the positive character qualities you observe in their lives. This will help alleviate the tendency to feel that if they had just been more perfect, the divorce would not have occurred.

Special Thoughts for Blended Families

1. Impact what, where, and when you can, then trust God with the rest. It's fruitless to try to control other home envi-

ronments. Focus on having oneness between parents in your home. Realize that differences and inconsistencies are almost inevitable between two home environments. If properly dealt with, these challenges can enhance a child's maturity. Challenging situations can mold a child's personal value system and deepen his or her convictions. Try not to fight the battle of insisting on common behaviors and rules for two homes, but focus on giving abundantly to a child's intimacy needs. This will help shape their behavior from the inside out.

2. A simple but very difficult task that every stepparent must face is loving their stepchild. Love begins with acceptance. Therefore, you may not experience all of the tender emotions that are present with a natural child, but acceptance of the stepchild is still our responsibility. Without the natural affection, you may have a tendency to focus solely on a stepchild's behavior. Avoid this tendency by finding positive character traits about each stepchild and then think of practical ways you can reinforce these traits. By changing your focus, you may begin to see the children with more accepting eyes. And as they sense your acceptance of who they are, their behavior may even change.

CHAPTER 4

Intimacy Ingredients...
A Recipe for Closeness

"DOORS LOCKED?"
  "Check."
  "Coffeepot off?"
  "Check."
  "Iron off?"
  "Check."
  "Electric rollers/curling iron off?"
  "Check."
  "Traveler's checks?"
  "Check."
  "Suitcases loaded?"
  "Check."
  "Gas tank full?"
  "Check."
  "Pressure in tires OK?"
  "Check."
  "Kids on board?"
  "Check."
  "Enough snacks to last us until the first pit stop?"
  "Check."
  "Checklist complete. Let's roll."

A Recipe for Closeness

Sounds like they're off to a good start, doesn't it? The operative word here is "start." Yes, all the necessary physical ingredients seem to be in place, but there's something missing. We'd like to suggest four emotional ingredients that are essential for the success of this parenting with intimacy journey.

Jesus said, "I came that they might have life, and might have it abundantly" (John 10:10). Surely He meant this for families as well as individuals. This, however, is not the whole of this oft-quoted verse. The first part warns, "The thief comes only to steal, and kill, and destroy." Satan is the archenemy of healthy family life. So, along with each essential ingredient for closeness, we'll also share a "Warning Sign" to alert you to Satan's roadblock.

Affectionate Caring

As a parent initiates verbal and physical affection, the child receives the important message, *"I care about you"* which translates into a sense of worth. This is "caught," not "taught" when you:

- Give your children your undivided attention as they share their thoughts, concerns, hurts, and dreams
- Prioritize time to talk, to enter their world
- Leave notes in strategic places that let them know they're special to you. Finding a note in a jacket pocket, lunch sack, or notebook that says, "I'll be thinking about you today" or "I'll be praying for you during your test" or "Have I told you lately what a great kid you are!" can bring an inner joy to your child guaranteed to last all day. Simple, yet heartwarming, these notes convey emotional attachment that builds closeness.
- Initiate an affectionate pat on the head or squeeze of the shoulder as you pass by, or give them a ten-second back scratch as you sit side-by-side while watching TV.
- Put your hand on her shoulder or arm around her waist while standing to sing a hymn in church or during the benediction. In a sense you're passing along your personal benediction or blessing. You're demonstrating to your child as well as those around you that "This is my beloved son or daughter, in whom I am well pleased."
- Hold hands as a family during prayers.

- Embrace as you go your separate ways in the morning and as you come back together later in the day. Anticipate his arrival home; don't make him search the house looking for you.
- Walk arm-in-arm or hand-in-hand through the mall.

Resist "backing off" affection as your child becomes a teenager. Of course, you'll want to be sensitive and "age-appropriate," but just because it becomes "uncool" to need parents doesn't mean their need for affection diminishes. In many ways, it increases as their sense of worth is threatened in other arenas.

"Warning Sign" . . . *Affectionate Caring is hindered by EMO-TIONAL BONDAGE*   Ephesians 4:31-32 tells us to "Let all bitterness and wrath and anger and clamor and slander be put away from you, along with all malice. And be kind to one another, tender-hearted, forgiving each other, just as God in Christ also has forgiven you." The bondage of anger, wrath, bitterness, and malice must be "put away" (turned loose of, emptied out of us) so that affectionate caring through kindness, tenderheartedness, and compassion can come forth. This warning underscores the importance of healing inevitable family hurts as father and mother role model confession to one another and to the children (1 John 1:9; James 5:16). As the Son sets us free, we will be "freed indeed" from these areas of bondage as a caring, compassionate life comes forth.

Vulnerable Communication

Vulnerability says *"I trust you."* A major ingredient in relational closeness is the open and constructive expression of emotion. This is the aspect in the relationship that risks transparency about feelings, needs, and hurts. If this level of communication is to occur, there must be a sense of security that home is a safe place to share without fear of further rejection, ridicule, or hurt. Trust is deepened as fears and dreams are shared in an atmosphere of respect and acceptance. Self-protective walls tumble as fear is "cast out" by the reassurance of "perfect love" (1 John 4:18-19).

Ask yourself these questions:

- Can feelings and needs be shared openly?
- Does my child feel safe in sharing hurts?
- Do I know what my child enjoys . . . what hurts?
- Is there an atmosphere in our home of acceptance and respect or one of lingering fear of criticism?

If you're feeling at this point like you may have just entered the "twilight zone," you're not alone. This realm of vulnerable communication is uncharted territory for many families. As you begin to explore new frontiers, start with small steps. For instance, take turns around the dinner table or during a fun family night together to answer these types of questions:

"I feel loved when _____"
"I feel hurt when _____"
"I feel scared when _____"

This sharing deepens openness and reveals specific clues regarding your child's areas of neediness and vulnerability. As parents vulnerably share their needs, hurts, and fears, children have their feelings and needs validated.

Hurts don't simply go away. Time doesn't spontaneously heal resentments and "trying harder" doesn't compensate for guilt. Here's a sobering thought: "My selfishness, or unloving attitude, or abusive words are why Christ had to die." As hurts are expressed, an opportunity arises to initiate the powerful healing tool of confession and forgiveness. Imagine the power of following this up with a time of vulnerable praying in which your child hears you asking God to enable you to be more patient, to give you the wisdom to know when to say no to outside commitments that take you away from time with your family, to make you more sensitive to their needs. As they "eavesdrop" on your conversation with God, their sense of worth skyrockets, their fears diminish, and their trust in God grows. We sometimes call this "perfect love" praying as a parent asks God to change her so as to more perfectly love her child; the child listens in and fear subsides.

"Warning Sign"... Vulnerable Communication is hindered by FEAR Satan plays to our weaknesses. He loves nothing better than for us to be bound by our fears. Fear of criticism, rejection, or inadequacy will hinder one's willingness to confront emotionally challenging situations. Fear of being hurt, disappointed, or used may cause one to seek to control all situations so as not to be vulnerable or "needy." But we don't have to allow Satan to steal, kill, and destroy. "For God has not given us a spirit of timidity [fear], but of power and love and discipline" (2 Tim. 1:7). "Perfect love casts out fear" (1 John 4:18). Parenting with intimacy requires a keen sensitivity to a child's journey through countless anxieties and fears—always ready to provide a reassuring word, comforting hug, and vulnerable prayer.

Joint Accomplishments

This ingredient in developing closeness says, *I need you* and comes from a feeling that WE did it! We're a team. As a team works together, their confidence is built and their sense of competency grows. A child's sense of confidence is directly affected by the number of things in which they feel competent. Feeling "unsure" of oneself and fighting self-doubt will undermine identity, stifle initiative, hinder motivation, and nourish despair. Good parenting doesn't delegate this realm to the school system or the church but begins early with practical, "real world" training. It will involve fun times with younger children—learning to tie shoes, play ball, pick out clothes, and ride bikes. Make these "family fun," not "solo" events. For older children and adolescents, it may involve "together" times of cooking, changing tires, writing thank-yous, sewing, shopping, and balancing checkbooks—just to name a few.

King Solomon, the writer of Proverbs, was one of the wisest men who ever lived. His keen observation that "where there is no vision, the people are unrestrained" (Prov. 29:18) lends credence to the importance of having a sense of direction and destiny.

Complaining that a high school graduate can't balance a

checkbook, wash clothes, write a letter, or make a long distance phone call is an indictment on parenting. Have a vision for training your children. This will involve taking the time to "show" them rather than just "tell" them. It's never too early (or too late) to start. This is so important we have devoted an entire chapter to "Preparing Your Children to Leave Home." Remember, competence grows in an atmosphere of praise and working together.

"Warning Sign" . . . *Joint Accomplishment is hindered by SELF-SUFFICIENCY* Satan's roadblock to the joy of joint accomplishment is seducing us into believing the notion that we have need of nothing and no one. It's difficult to sense "closeness" to a person who has no apparent needs. This air of self-sufficiency keeps others at arm's length and short-circuits attempts to develop intimacy. Too often, family members are left to tackle life's challenges *alone*, each busy with their own agenda and struggles—robbed of the blessing of sharing the journey together. Such self-sufficiency often develops through prolonged periods of unmet needs and the associated hurt which "drives" a person to deny their needs or turn to self-nurturing ways to meet them (eating, workaholism, perfectionism, and other escapes). The promise found in Philippians 4:19, "And my God shall supply all your needs according to His riches in glory in Christ Jesus" bulldozes right through this roadblock of self-sufficiency! This verse clearly reminds us that we do have needs. An added reminder to parents is that God's plan to supply your child's needs much of the time involves YOU as His intended source of provision.

Mutual Giving

This ingredient for closeness says, *"I love you"* as the focus is on *giving to* rather than *taking from* one another. Children need adults who are willing to model this type of selfless giving. It truly is "more blessed to give than to receive" (Acts 20:35). We all come into life in our "fallen" state, fearful of receiving, and so we "take" from others.

Parents who prioritize the initiative to "give" to their child's needs are again ministering perfect love to address this fear and role modeling to the child the blessing of giving. In contrast, nothing quenches intimacy faster than feeling "taken" from . . . or taken for granted. Children can experience this pain when they are exhorted to act right, "help out," and "be nice" — while no one seems to be taking time just for them. No one seems to really know them. "Taking" is characterized by a very conditional love that says, "I'll love you if" or "I'll love you when. . . . " A relationship characterized by "taking" will soon show signs of resentment, discouragement, and distance. If we take from one another in an attempt to meet our needs, there's no fulfillment or satisfaction. There's a difference between "taking" a hug and being lovingly "given" one!

"Warning Sign" . . . Mutual Giving is hindered by SELFISHNESS This should come as no great surprise. Selfishness is consistent with our self-centered "natural" state. However, through a personal relationship with Christ we have available a new resource and strength to give rather than take. It's still a choice, though. Which path will you travel — the broad one of taking, or the narrow one of giving that leads to life. The Apostle Paul urges us down the narrow path, "Do nothing from selfishness or empty conceit, but with humility of mind let each of you regard one another as more important than himself; do not merely look out for your own personal interests, but also for the interests of others" (Phil. 2:3-4).

Mix Well

As with any recipe, it's not enough just to have the right ingredients, they have to be mixed together so the flavors can blend and the proper chemistry take place. Our four essential ingredients of affectionate caring, vulnerable communication, joint accomplishment, and mutual giving must now be stirred. The instrument we need to stir them properly is a skill we call "Emotional Responding."

Emotional needs call for an emotional response. Sounds reasonable, even simple, but more often than not we tend to respond to emotional needs with:

- Facts/Logic/Reason/Advice
- Criticism
- Complaints (My Hurt/Need)
- Neglect

These responses are guaranteed to "miss" the target. Rather than applying a soothing salve to heal the emotional wound, they serve instead to cut even deeper.

As an adolescent, Lance went through a "chubby stage." His peers at school taunted him with names like "pound cake" and "fatso." Whenever he shared his hurt with his parents, he received such unproductive responses as:

"This is just a stage you're going through. You won't always be fat. Besides, kids will always find a reason to tease you." (Logic/Reason)

"I have a great diet for you to try." (Advice)

"If you wouldn't eat so much you wouldn't be fat. If you just wouldn't put so much sugar in your tea. . . ." (Criticism)

"People always made fun of me, especially about my height. When I was growing up they called me "stump" or "shorty." (Complaint . . . Focus on Parent's Hurt)

"Just focus on something positive." (Neglect)

None of these "connected" with Lance's emotional need. He needed comfort. He needed his parents to feel his hurt and "enter into" his suffering so that he would not have to endure it alone. He needed to hear something like, "I can imagine how much that teasing must hurt. It makes me sad to see you hurting. I want you to know that I'm here for you."

For emotional closeness to occur, family members must learn to express emotion and communicate with feelings. This is difficult for many of us to do because we grew up without a "feeling vocabulary."

As you develop your feeling vocabulary, the next step is to learn to answer emotion with emotion. Here are some examples of what this looks and sounds like.

"I can see that you're hurting (or sad, or scared, or _____)."

"It saddens me that you feel so alone at school."

"I can see how disappointed you are that you weren't invited to the party. I want you to know that I care."

"I can appreciate that you're upset about missing the game. I know that's disappointing to you."

"I know you're really frustrated right now because you're having trouble understanding algebra. I want you to know that I care about you and will help you in any way I can."

"I know you're anxious about this big exam. I want you to know I'll be praying for you. I love you!"

"I'm committed to going through this with you."

"Can you share with me how I've hurt you? . . . and how it made you feel? I want to understand and make it right."

"I see that I hurt you by my _____ and that was wrong of me. Will you forgive me?"

As you allow your heart to feel what your head knows and then communicate that to your child, you become a channel of comfort and blessing. Ephesians 4:29 actually speaks of us ministering God's grace as we share words that edify. Language is a powerful gift from God. It allows us to worship God, communicate information with one another, and fully express emotions. Proverbs speaks to the power and impact of our words and their power to heal.

"A soothing tongue is a tree of life
   but a perversion in it crushes the spirit" (Prov. 15:4).
"Death and life are in the power of the tongue" (Prov. 18:21).
"Pleasant words are a honeycomb, sweet to the soul and healing to the bones" (Prov. 16:24).
"Anxiety in the heart of a man weighs it down,
   but a good word makes it glad" (Prov. 12:25).

Mix Well . . . and Serve

We've mixed our ingredients well. Now it's time to serve. Ask the Lord to empower you to serve Him and one another.

For you were called to freedom, brethren; only do not turn your freedom into an opportunity for the flesh, but through love serve one another.

Galatians 5:13

Ask Yourself

1. Do you and your children have an adequate feeling vocabulary? Are you able to identify when you are feeling happy, sad, angry, or afraid? Before you can begin to share a closeness in family relationships, there must be an awareness of feelings and emotions. These feelings need to have labels attached to them so they can be communicated.

Develop a list of feeling words with your children. According to age-level, make the task of increasing the feeling vocabulary a fun part of life. Identify feelings of television characters, *Mickey is sad because he misses his parents.* Look through magazines at the doctor's office. Match feeling words with the faces. Before bedtime, discuss the events of the day and the feelings associated with them. *How did you feel when you caught that pass during practice? How do you think Elizabeth felt when you told her you weren't going to play with her anymore?*

2. Give every family member the opportunity to complete the sentence, *I feel cared about when . . .* or *I feel loved when . . .* Listen attentively. The responses may be different from your own. They may even be different from what you expect. Once this preference has been verbalized, don't ridicule, correct, or suggest alternatives—no matter how inconsequential it may seem to you. How can you meet this verbalized need for each child? Even in this simple exercise, how do your children show their uniqueness?

Experiencing Truth

John 13:14 "If I then, the Lord and the Teacher, have washed your feet, you also ought to wash one another's." Serving others with sensitivity and initiative is critical to deepening relationships. Christ exemplifies this in His

EMOTIONAL RESPONDING

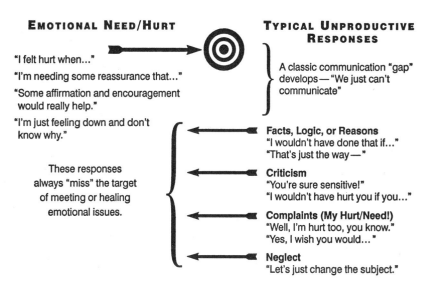

EMOTIONAL NEED/HURT

"I felt hurt when..."

"I'm needing some reassurance that..."

"Some affirmation and encouragement would really help."

"I'm just feeling down and don't know why."

These responses always "miss" the target of meeting or healing emotional issues.

TYPICAL UNPRODUCTIVE RESPONSES

A classic communication "gap" develops — "We just can't communicate"

Facts, Logic, or Reasons
"I wouldn't have done that if..."
"That's just the way —"

Criticism
"You're sure sensitive!"
"I wouldn't have hurt you if you..."

Complaints (My Hurt/Need!)
"Well, I'm hurt too, you know."
"Yes, I wish you would... "

Neglect
"Let's just change the subject."

Characteristic of fulfilled or "healthy" relationships is learning to respond "emotionally." Noted in the chart below are illustrations of productive responses to emotional need or hurt.

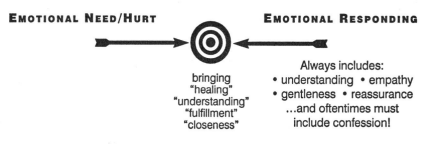

EMOTIONAL NEED/HURT

bringing
"healing"
"understanding"
"fulfillment"
"closeness"

EMOTIONAL RESPONDING

Always includes:
• understanding • empathy
• gentleness • reassurance
...and oftentimes must
include confession!

Example Productive Emotional Responses

"I can really see that you're hurting (or_____)."

"I don't like to see you hurting."

"It saddens me to see you so fearful (or_____)."

"I deeply care about you and love you."

"I'm committed to go through this with you."

"I genuinely regret my part in hurting you."

"Can you share with me how I've hurt you?...And how it made you feel? I want to understand and make it right."

"I now see that I hurt you by my _____ and that was wrong of me...will you forgive me?"

washing of the disciples' feet. First He was sensitive to their need; He noticed other's needs around Him. Second, He took initiative to give to the needs. Jesus didn't wait for the disciples to ask. Try praying and living this request: *Heavenly Father, I want to be a better servant to my family. Help me this week, lift my focus beyond myself to notice the needs of others; prompt and empower my initiative in giving to meet these needs.*

Special Thoughts for Single Parents

Remember that sharing experiences with your child is the mortar that holds the relationship together. It means sharing the little experiences, both good and bad — breakfast at McDonald's, learning to bowl, getting lost on the way to the game. It also means sharing the big experiences — getting a driver's license, losing a family pet, or the first day of school. You have the opportunities to talk to your child, hold your child, and touch her life. Don't beat yourself up for what you can't do. Don't get hung up on what you don't have. Give yourself permission to be one parent, not both. If you will invest even small amounts of purposeful time and energy into meeting your child's emotional needs, the impact will be dramatic. Carefully set aside time to give your child the ingredients of care, trust, joint accomplishment, and love. Focusing on these ingredients will maximize your efforts as a single parent.

Special Thoughts for Blended Families

Increase the intimacy ingredients of care and love as you show respect for others. In a family where children and adults may be adjusting to new living arrangements, different routines, and a lack of privacy, the need for respect becomes paramount. Do you knock before entering a room? Do you ask for feedback on decisions that affect everyone? Do you show respect for the parent who is not in your home? Do you allow transitional objects (mementos from the other parent) into your home? Do you practice thoughtfulness and common courtesy with the other parent or family?

CHAPTER 5

Freedom to Be a Parent... Leaving Behind Your Own Childhood

WEIGH STATION AHEAD . . . Be Prepared to Stop! We've all seen the sign as we've barreled down the expressway. But, unless you happen to be a truck driver, you've dismissed it as not applying to you and kept on going. Not this time. We're all pulling in to check our loads. And what we're likely to find is that we're hauling some extra poundage that needs to be lightened.

It's crystal clear throughout Scripture that God is a God of order in every facet of His creation, including marriage and family. The first biblical reference to marriage is found in Genesis 2:24, "For this cause *[marriage]* a man shall leave his father and his mother, and shall cleave to his wife; and they shall become one flesh." Two chapters later Adam and Eve bring forth children and begin their parenting journey. That's God's order: We leave father and mother; cleave unto one another; become intimate with one another—physically, emotionally, and spiritually—and THEN we're ready to be parents.

As you pull into the weigh station, you may find yourself faced with a dilemma. You may discover you've reversed the order. You're already a parent, but you haven't finished leaving. There are still some things left unresolved from your own growing up experience that are impacting your ability to parent. For instance, as you're challenged to give your child attention and enter into his world, what if your mom and dad were too busy to enter into your world? The person who really knew you was the baby-sitter. Every day after school you'd sit and talk to her while she ironed. She was the only one who ever really listened to you. Or, if not the baby-sitter, maybe that person was a teacher or a high school coach. Your child desperately craves approval, but you never received it and aren't sure how to give it—what it looks or sounds like. Or, as you're called upon to comfort your child through the inevitable disappointments, defeats, and misunderstandings of life, you come to grips with the fact that as you were growing up you hurt alone. What now? You cannot give to your children what you don't possess. Eventually your gauge will reflect "E" and you'll have to pull to the side of the road to have your own tank filled.

David and Teresa found themselves in much the same situation. They had been pretty much in agreement on how to raise their two daughters, Terri and Robin. But an interesting dynamic kicked in when their son, Eric, came along. They began to diverge in their parenting approach. David found it very hard, if not impossible, to say no to Eric . . . but, not to worry, Teresa was there to pick up the slack! Her motto was "Nip it in the bud." The more she nipped, the more David slacked off, feeling sorry for "poor Eric." The more David slacked off, the more Teresa nipped. And so it went. They became increasingly polarized in their parenting. David admits that in spite of his "several degrees in this area," it took him awhile to figure out what was going on. It all came into focus one Saturday morning.

The Case of the Lone Begonia

Spring had sprung at the Ferguson's. It was time to get out into the yard and get things cleaned up. Teresa, lover of the great outdoors, was in her glory. David, lover of the great indoors, was not. Everyone had an assigned task and went about their business. Ten-year-old Eric was assigned to the dead plant detail in the front yard. He was to dig up the plants that had died over the winter. Simple, direct, manageable.

After some time had passed, David decided to go around to the front to see how Eric was coming along. His findings? One dug-up begonia, one shovel, one missing bike—and one missing Eric. Let's let David tell it from here.

"It never occurred to me to go find him, bring him back, and discipline him. I actually walked over, picked up the shovel, and began to dig up the rest of those dead plants. Instead of thinking about what would be an appropriate consequence for his behavior, I'm thinking, 'I'd better hurry up and finish digging up these plants before Teresa catches me doing it!' I have enough degrees to know this is pathological! I was enabling Eric's irresponsibility and trying to do it as quickly as possible before I got caught."

Asking the Lord for wisdom and applying his academic training, David gained insight into the dynamics of what was taking place. What was going on with Eric hadn't surfaced with Terri or Robin. There was a fear inside of David that said something like this: "At all costs, I don't want my son feeling about me some of the things I felt about my dad growing up. At all costs, as my son's growing up, I want him to like me." And David had concluded somewhere along the way because of his own unresolved issues from childhood that this meant he couldn't tell Eric no or be strict with him.

David determined in his heart that he had to talk to Eric. He confessed to him that he had hurt him by enabling his irresponsibility. He actually apologized to him and asked for his forgiveness. He apologized to Teresa for his lack of support, and together they explored David's growing-up pain. In the days that followed David began to be more strict with Eric and to use that much-feared no word, even though it was still extremely hard.

About a month after their conversation, Eric was late getting up one morning and was running around the house trying to get ready for school. Unable to find his own toothpaste, he rushed into David's bathroom, squeezed some of David's toothpaste onto his brush, and was about to walk off leaving the toothpaste on the counter with the cap still off. David summoned every bit of strength and faith he had as he said, "Buddy, you need to come back and put up the toothpaste." That may not sound like a big deal, but it was for David because of his fear that Eric wouldn't like him.

Eric came back, replaced the cap and, never one to be at a loss for words, looked back at his dad with an impish grin and said, "Dad, I still like you!"

Facing the Hurt

In our heart-of-hearts, we can all say, "We've been there!" The hurt, the fear, the circumstance will vary, but most of us have been hindered in our parenting journey by unresolved childhood issues. Although we don't claim to be psychic, we are confident we can tell you three things about yourself:

- As you were growing up, you were an imperfect person
- You grew up in an imperfect environment
- You had imperfect people around you

We know, beyond a shadow of a doubt, that these things are true because you're human. And all human beings are imperfect, no exceptions other than the God-man Jesus! A natural consequence of the interaction of these three truths is that you have experienced dimensions of hurt. Before you get defensive ("But my parents did the best they could!"), we need to separate out motives and methods. A parent can have great motives, "I love you. I care about you. I want what's best for you" but at the same time employ methods that are hurtful. If someone accidentally drops a heavy rock on your foot, it still hurts even though it was unintentional. Acknowledging pain doesn't translate into assigning blame. We must come to see that it involves the pursuit of truth.

As is the case with most boys his age, making his bed wasn't a high priority with David. After all, he was going to be crawling right back under those covers in another twelve hours, give or take a few. So, what was the point? Well, to his Marine drill sergeant father, the point (*motive*) was teaching David responsibility and that a job worth doing was worth doing well. So, at "inspection," if the quarter didn't bounce high enough the sheets came off and David started over . . . and over . . . and over. This sometimes took an hour out of a perfectly good Saturday morning! And, David's need for his father's approval went unmet. In later years, David and his dad were able to talk about such things and resolve the hurt. As a critical part of a healthy "leaving" process, with great maturity his dad came to acknowledge that while his motives were good, his methods brought pain. The pain was addressed, healed, and a much enriched relationship ensued.

Additionally painful in the lives of many is when not only were parents' methods wrong, but their "motives" were wrong as well—as in the case of abuse, incest, and related traumas. This dual pain of both motives and methods will require additional grief and comfort work as covered in this chapter.

The question is not, "Have you experienced hurt?" That's a foregone conclusion. We've all been undernourished in some areas of need and the result is hurt. The question is, "Has the hurt been faced? Has it been healed?" Facing hurt head-on leads to opportunities for growth. Denial, on the other hand, stunts growth. Tragically, it's not uncommon to hear statements like,

"No, I never heard anyone tell me they were proud of me, but it's no big deal."

"No, I never heard my dad actually say he loved me, but that's just the way he was. It didn't really hurt me."

"I'm not sure I could honestly say anyone knew me—not really deep-down. But, hey, I did OK without it."

This may sound harsh, but those statements just cannot be true, and they represent emotional bondage. John 8:32, speaking specifically of God's Word, and more broadly of God's truth, says, "You shall know the truth, and the truth shall make you free." If you're going to find freedom and help your children find it, you're going to have to confront and deal with the truth about your own childhood.

At this juncture you may be thinking, "But doesn't Scripture teach that we're supposed to honor our parents? It seems like if I identify areas in which I experienced hurt growing up, that this would be dishonoring them."

Not at all! You're honoring them by coming to grips with the truth and committing yourself to growth. What could be more honoring to a parent than for their child to live a life of integrity in which he strives to become all he can be for Jesus Christ! Truth and trust are the cornerstone of relationships. It's true that in every human relationship positive things occur and painful things occur. The only relationship that is totally positive is divine, and even that relationship involves "pain" in terms of God's discipline in our lives which we experience as painful at times. Pain is part of life.

Truly honoring your father and mother means recognizing the pain that was also present in their lives that perhaps hindered them in their ability to meet some of your needs. You honor them as you allow them to come down off a pedestal that keeps them out of reach. You honor them as you allow them to be human beings who made (and make!) mistakes. You can only truly honor a "real" person, not an "imaginary" one. One can't really come to a full appreciation of the blessings they received from their parents without also acknowledging and healing the hurts. In essence, blockading the hurts blockades the blessings as well.

Remember, an integral part of every child's developmental journey is coming to grips with the fact that her parents were not (and are not) perfect. If you're unwilling to wrestle with this truth, you're destined to be on a never-ending, unachievable personal quest to be a perfect parent yourself. And your children will suffer because of it.

DISHONOR CASTS BLAME.
HONOR EMBRACES TRUTH.

Establish What Is to Be Forgiven

You'll never be any more sensitive to other's needs and hurts than you are to your own! This won't mean you become "self-focused" but rather you'll become more real, transparent, and approachable, more compassionate, and actually more "others-focused."

So, it's time to put down your reflector shield and conduct an honest self-appraisal.

How would you answer the question, "I feel really cared about by my spouse when he or she _____"? Feel free to give as many answers as come to mind. Then try to identify the related need. For example:

"When he puts down the newspaper and listens to what I'm saying." (Attention)

"When she builds me up in front of the kids." (Approval/Respect)

"When he hugs me and tells me he loves me for no special reason." (Affection)

"When she lets me blow off steam without trying to solve the problem." (Comfort)

Your answer(s) likely have deep roots in your childhood. Answers typically fall into one of two categories. Either they reveal a need that was abundantly met as you were growing up and you connected it with love. Or, you really missed that and came into marriage hoping your spouse would have a vital part in ministering to that need.

In chapter 1 we identified the top ten intimacy needs and asked you to do a needs assessment for each of your children. Now the focus is on you. Listed on the next page are those ten needs along with a number of others. With your commitment to facing the truth securely in tow, prioritize a quiet, reflective time to review this list and mark it like this. If this need was met by your dad, give yourself a half-circle ["("]. If you received this from your mom, give yourself the other half-circle [")"]. If you received it from both of them, you'll have a full-circle ["()"]. As you go through the list, you may find some needs that you missed altogether. Mark those with an "X."

After you've completed the list, begin journaling some of your reflections. You may find it a struggle to write about your own pain. Ephesians 4:31 says to "put away anger, wrath and bitterness." You can only "put away" what you

Understanding Intimacy Needs

"freely you have received . . . therefore freely give"
— **Matthew 10:8**

*A*new commandment I give to you, that you love one another, even as I have loved you, that you also love one another.
—John 13:34

Scripture is filled with these "one another" passages which focus on giving to another. Each contains an admonition to give, but also a need which others must have. A study of these one-another passages gives insight into God-created needs which we have opportunity to meet.

A Recent Survey of Top 10 Needs

- Attention
- Acceptance
- Appreciation
- Support
- Encouragement
- Affection
- Approval
- Security
- Comfort
- Respect

Gratefulness for God's abundant and gracious provision to me prompts me to a stewardship of giving to the needs of others (Rom. 5:17; 1 Peter 4:10).

As each one has received . . . serve one another as good stewards of the manifold grace of God."

1. **ACCEPTANCE** — deliberate and ready reception with favorable positive response — (Rom. 15:7)
2. **ADMONITION** — constructive guidance in what to avoid . . . to warn — (Rom. 15:14)
3. **AFFECTION (Greet with a Kiss)** — to communicate care and closeness through physical touch and loving words — (Rom. 16:16)
4. **APPRECIATION (Praise)** — to communicate with words and feeling personal gratefulness for another — (1 Cor. 11:2)
5. **APPROVAL** — expressed commendation; to think and speak well of — (Rom. 14:18)
6. **ATTENTION (Care)** — to take thought of another and convey appropriate interest, support, etc.; to enter into another's "world" — (1 Cor. 12:25)

7. **COMFORT (Empathy)** — to come alongside with word, feeling, and touch; to give consolation with tenderness — (1 Thes. 4:18)
8. **COMPASSION** — to suffer with and through another in trial/burden — (Heb. 10:34)
9. **CONFESSION** — open acknowledgment of wrongs committed based upon inner conviction — (James 5:16)
10. **DEFERENCE (Subject)** — to yield or defer oneself to another for their benefit — (Eph. 5:21)
11. **DEVOTION** — a firm and dependable foundation of committed care — (Rom. 12:10)
12. **DISCIPLINE** — to reprove and correct when boundaries are crossed and limits exceeded — (Prov. 23:13; Rev. 3:19)
13. **EDIFICATION (Build Up)** — to positively promote the growth and development of another — (Rom. 14:19)
14. **ENCOURAGEMENT** — to urge forward and positively persuade toward a goal — (1 Thes. 5:11; Heb. 10:24)
15. **FORGIVENESS** — to cancel out or "release" wrongs committed and bestow instead unconditional favor — (Eph. 4:32)
16. **HARMONY** — an environment of pleasant acceptance and secure love — (1 Peter 3:8)
17. **HOSPITALITY** — open reception of another with a loving heart — (1 Peter 4:9)
18. **INTIMACY (Fellowship)** — deep sharing and communion with another as lives are shared in "common" — (1 John 1:7)
19. **KINDNESS** — pleasant and gracious servanthood — (Eph. 4:32)
20. **LOVE** — seeking welfare of others and opportunity to "do good"; consistent with having first been loved by God and seeing His value of others, the characteristic Word of Christianity — (John 13:34)
21. **PRAYER** — to entreat God's attention and favor . . . upon another — (James 5:16)
22. **RESPECT (Honor)** — to value and regard highly; to convey great worth — (Rom. 12:10)
23. **SECURITY (Peace)** — confidence of "harmony" in relationship; free from harm — (Mark 9:50)
24. **SENSITIVE (Same Mind)** — seeking to understand and accept another without judging — (Rom. 12:16)
25. **SERVE** — giving up of oneself in caring ministry to another — (Gal. 5:13)
26. **SUPPORT (Bear Burdens)** — come alongside and gently help carry a load (problem, struggle) — (Gal. 6:2)
27. **SYMPATHY** — to identify with another "emotionally" — (1 Peter 3:8)
28. **TEACHING** — constructive and positive instruction in how to live — (Col. 3:16)
29. **TRAINING (Equip)** — journey with me to model God's way of facing life's issues — (Luke 6:40)
30. **UNDERSTANDING (Forbearance)** — patient endurance of another's humanness — (Eph. 4:2; Col. 3:13)

acknowledge you have. So avoid "explaining away" or "minimizing" the hurt. Just write your feelings—sorrows as well as joys. Healing begins at the point of establishing and facing the pain.

Grieve the Loss

Allow yourself to grieve the "loss" associated with the pain. It will be helpful to remember specific hurts—events when you needed comfort and missed it; you needed approval but no one noticed; you needed attention or affection and important people in your life did not provide it. To grieve is to focus on the emotions behind your loss—just as you would grieve over the loss of a loved one. Continue journaling your "feelings." It might be helpful to refer back to page 85 in the last chapter. Can you identify that— "I felt" or "I feel" . . . lonely . . . sad . . . afraid . . . angry . . . disappointed . . . unloved . . . violated . . . unimportant . . . etc.?

Don't expect to move through this quickly. Grieving is a process, not a once-for-all exercise. As experiences and situations arise that bring to mind the hurt again, allow yourself to grieve.

Receive Comfort

"Blessed are those who mourn, for they shall be comforted" (Matt. 5:4). God desires to comfort your grief . . . and He often will use other people. Identify a special "journey-mate" to share in your grief. This might be a spouse, pastor, counselor, or a special friend within the body of Christ. If you're married, the most "blessed" comfort will come from your spouse—so if at all possible involve him or her. Allow this person to "journey" with you in sharing your grief and ministering comfort. You might want to read from your journal or talk about your feelings concerning what you missed and how you felt. Share what you need from them. "I have something I'd like to share with you about some of my hurts and feelings. As I do, I just need you to listen."

Or, "I could sure use a hug right now." Allow them to feel sad about your hurt and to hurt with you. As you are comforted, you will, in turn, be able to minister comfort to others. For the journeymate who provides comfort, it may be helpful to review the material on "Emotional Responding" in chapter 4 where specific examples are given of what comfort "sounds like."

> *Blessed be the God and Father of our Lord Jesus Christ,*
> *the Father of mercies and God of all comfort;*
> *who comforts us in all our affliction so that we*
> *may be able to comfort those who are in any affliction*
> *with the comfort with which we ourselves are comforted by God.*
> *2 Corinthians 1:3-4*

Ask Yourself

1. You will never be any more sensitive to others' needs than you are to your own. Take time to do your own needs assessment. While thinking about the list of ten intimacy needs, complete these statements: "I feel loved when . . . " "When I was growing up, I missed . . . " and "Now that I am an adult, I realize that I need more . . . " Share these responses with your spouse or journeymate.

How might your increased awareness of unmet needs affect your relationship with your children?

2. Consider the biblical concept of "leaving your father and mother." In what ways has this taken place in your life? Resist these two extremes: (1) Have you denied the imperfections of your parents? The most appropriate way to honor your parents is to come to grips with the truth. In spite of loving motives, all parents at times use imperfect methods. (2) Are you stuck in the trap of blaming your parents? We all received some childhood hurts for which we are not responsible, but we are accountable for our response to that hurt. Have you chosen the path of healing and forgiveness?

Experiencing Truth

Second Corinthians 1:3-4 speaks of the "God of all comfort;

who comforts us in all our affliction, so that we may be able to comfort those who are in any affliction." Take your unmet needs to the great Comforter. Let God know the hurts that resulted from an imperfect world. Let Him know what you missed and how that felt. What do you need from God? Have you been still long enough to hear His loving response? Have you been honest with God about your feelings and experiences? Have you been receptive to His comfort? Will you allow Him to additionally provide His comfort through a journeymate who cares for you?

Special Thoughts for Single Parents

Be careful to finish your own emotional grief work. Individuals who have gone through a divorce or death of a spouse have many grief issues. It will be important for you to identify any unresolved losses so that you will be free to respond adequately to your children. With a trusted friend, counselor, or journeymate work to identify your own feelings, hurts, and losses. Your sensitivity to your own struggles will increase your sensitivity to your children. If you minimize your own pain, you will tend to minimize the hurts of your child. If you get stuck in your own pain and don't move past it, your children may begin to feel responsible for your feelings or happiness.

Special Thoughts for Blended Families

You and your spouse may find it necessary to spend some time grieving the loss of the "perfect family" and comforting one another. As with any family, the blended family must face the positive and negative experiences that go along with relationships. Don't deny the challenges of blending two families, but focus on the opportunities you have together.

You and your partner may be reluctant to look back at the past hurts of childhood. There is a mistaken tendency to ignore the past and press on toward the future. But coming to terms with the hurts of your own childhood will allow you to bring resolution to that pain.

CHAPTER 6

Getting to Know Your Child…
Little Is Much When God Is in It

TODAY WE KNOW more "about" children, teenagers, and families than we've ever known in the history of time. We have at our fingertips more research than we could assimilate in a lifetime and unlimited access to the Information Super Highway. Yet, we seem to have more problems than ever. How can this be? It's not enough just to know *about* kids. We must know *our* kids and help them know themselves. This happens within the confines of relationships.

In order for a child to grow up, this equation must be in place:

ROLES ➤ RELATIONSHIPS ➤ GROWTH

Children don't grow up by reading a book or watching TV. They grow up in the context of relationships in which each person is in his proper role. This means adults must be willing to be adults—and free enough from their own childhood to respond like adults. Kids are not asked to shoulder adult responsibilities, and moms and dads don't act like children. Moms are moms. Dads are dads. Kids are kids.

Sadly, relationships are often painted in harsh strokes of black and white, reduced to sets of rules and regulations. Certainly those things are important. Teaching children to be responsible for themselves is part of the parenting process. But there is so much more. As you put your hand in your child's and guide him in painting his life's landscape, use the vast array of colors God has made available to you. Each child is a masterpiece in the making, revealed one brush stroke at a time.

It's the Little Things That Count

This truth was brought home to Paul early in his training through one of God's choice servants. Mama Jean had a divine calling. She opened her home and her heart to some of Dallas' most difficult kids. Over the years, she had provided foster care for kids deemed "unreachable" by others of less stalwart determination.

Part of the training for the interns and residents was to spend time evaluating some of Mama Jean's techniques. One day as they sat talking during an uncharacteristic lull in the action, one of them asked, "Mama Jean, what's the key? What's the most important thing to remember in taking care of kids? You've raised hundreds of them . . . and not just any kids . . . the tough ones. What's your secret?"

A gentle smile spread across her wise face. They braced themselves for the pearls of wisdom to come, fully expecting a psychological treatise of some sort.

"Well, I'll tell you what I've learned over the years. It's actually in a song that I learned when I was a little girl. The chorus goes like this. "Little is much when God is in it, Labor not for wealth or fame; There's a crown and you can win it, if you go in Jesus' name."

Parenting isn't about amassing wealth or fame. It's about faithfulness in the little things. It's about getting to know your child. Several years ago a pastor shared his heart with David. "I'm so proud of my daughter's walk with the Lord. She's a disciplined Christian young lady. She has a quiet time every day and shares her faith with her friends. It's exciting to see her take a stand on the tough issues, and she's loyal to her family and friends. I'm thrilled to see that she's believing right and behaving right. But there seems to be something missing in our relationship. David, I'm not sure that I really know her."

Teaching our children to believe right and behave right is important. Essential, in fact. But not sufficient. The Apostle Paul put it this way, "We were well pleased to impart to you not only the Gospel . . . but also our own lives" (1 Thes. 2:8). Sometimes we try to make this more

complicated than it is. God has equipped you with everything you need. As you travel this road of discovery, use your
God-given senses (and sense!) to get to know your child.

Watch

Keep your eyes open. Watch your children—not to be entertained (although that may happen!)—but to look for
clues to unlock what's going on inside of them.

Mr. Johnson, the superintendent of Luke's Sunday
School department, was at his wit's end. Luke's behavior
had become almost unmanageable. Chronically angry,
Luke literally hissed at his teacher whenever asked to do
anything he didn't want to do. He had no friends at
church—not surprising considering the way he picked
fights. Mr. Johnson had tried to talk to Luke one-on-one
on several occasions, but to no avail. Each time Luke refused to make eye contact and constantly fiddled with
something in his pocket. Mr. Johnson found this annoying,
interpreting it as lack of respect and inattention. Finally,
he asked, "Luke, what's in your pocket?"

Luke raised his head and a shy smile crept across his
face. He pulled an action figure from his pocket. "This is
King David. He killed a giant, you know! I keep him in my
pocket because he was a brave soldier. I keep thinking that
maybe if I keep him in my pocket and hold him once in a
while, maybe I won't be so scared all the time. Kids make
fun of me and I don't have any friends. I get in trouble all
the time at school and here at church . . . and, well, I just
feel angry and scared all the time."

It was a beginning! Mr. Johnson had opened a window
into Luke's heart by watching what he was doing. As you
watch your own child, keep in mind that "You won't know
what's in their heart if you don't know what's in their pocket!"

Listen

We want our kids to respect us; they desire our respect as
well. The best place to start is to listen to what they have to

say. When you listen intently, you'll hear what they're really saying. Most of the time, we adults assume we know what kids think, feel, and are going to say about something so we just pretend to be listening while we formulate our comeback. Another interesting benefit of listening is that if adults would stop and listen (not necessarily agree with, but listen) eventually kids will begin to listen to themselves. Too often, exasperated adults skip the listening stage and jump straight to arguing. As the ranting and raving escalates, no one's listening.

This was the case with Peter and his parents. Peter just had to have a car. Not just any car, a brand-new Jeep Cherokee. He argued incessantly. "I deserve it. You can afford it. What do you do with your money anyway?" His parents were totally turned off by his demanding spirit. The three of them ranted and raved, sometimes individually and sometimes simultaneously. It's a wonder their "discussions" didn't register on the Richter scale! Seeing they were getting nowhere, and possibly going in reverse, Peter's parents tried a different strategy. One night at the dinner table, they decided to just let Peter pontificate uninterrupted. After about ten minutes, he stopped in his tracks. His eyes welled up with tears. "You know what? What I'm really trying to tell you is that I feel so unsure of myself and so lonely at school that I think if I had a car maybe everything would be different."

We're not advocating just letting your child go on and on every time, but if you've been watching . . . and listening . . . looking for clues . . . you'll know when the time is right.

Communicate

In the end, communication is probably your most important tool in gaining an understanding of what's going on inside of your child. But it's imperative that you first establish your interest in them by watching and listening. Kids often turn off to their parents because they feel like they're constantly forcing them to "communicate" and bugging them if they don't talk. One of the keys in getting your kids to talk to you is giving them permission not to talk. Ninety-nine percent of the time this works like magic.

Say what you mean, and mean what you say. No empty threats. This goes for parents and kids alike. Don't say things you don't mean, even when you're frustrated. "I've had it with you! You're grounded for the next two years!" You both know that's not going to happen. No asking questions if there's not really a question. No giving choices if there is no choice. "Would you like to clean up your room now?" Any red-blooded American kid, especially a boy, is going to answer, "Not really." Then Mom or Dad gets mad because it never really was a choice. And don't end sentences with, "OK?" if it's not an option. "It's time to get ready for bed now, OK?" "It's time for your bath now, OK?" Here's a more painful example of the impact of what you say. "If you ever did that, I would just die." Do you suppose your child will come to you if they've done "that" after they've heard you say it would kill you? Say what you mean, and mean what you say.

Use the correct punctuation and a mixture of punctuation when talking to your kids. This will go a long way in holding their attention. Have you ever gotten a letter that had no punctuation? It just runs on and on, and you eventually lose interest because it's just too hard to decipher. Similarly, if you punctuate every sentence with a question mark your kids will tune you out. Where are you going? When will you be back? What did you do? Who was there? Why didn't you call? Will you ever learn? Using all periods is called lecturing. It's boring, and kids hate it! And we've all been in conversations (shouting matches?) where the only punctuation is exclamation points. Sit down! Be quiet! I've had it with you! Go to your room! Wait until your father gets home! Show your kids you were paying attention in English class. Mix up your punctuation and just maybe they'll listen.

The last, and perhaps most important, rule of communication is *don't mind read.* Don't try to read theirs and don't expect them to read yours. It's a surefire way to cripple a growing relationship and destroy intimacy.

Think

It's easy sometimes to lapse into an automatic pilot mode, putting our brains in neutral. Stay alert. Always be thinking about what's going on. Akin to "watching," this involves developing a mind-set that says there are no accidents—no coincidences. You don't "accidentally" find out your child has done something. You don't "accidentally" find a note your teenager has left lying around or "accidentally" find cigarettes (or worse!) in your son's shirt pocket. There's a reason. Part of that reason is that God wants you involved in your child's life, and the other part is that your child wants you involved—even if it doesn't seem like it. Determine in your heart to aim higher than just labeling and attempting to "straighten out" behavior. Search for the *whys* behind the behavior. Keep in mind, there are needs beneath every deed.

Watching . . . Listening . . . Communicating . . . Thinking . . . These are keys that will unlock the treasure that is your child. They don't cost a thing . . . except time.

A Precious Commodity

In the '50s, '60s, and '70s the "quality versus quantity" camps squabbled over which reigned supreme. It's really a no-brainer. Any kid will tell you there's no such thing as quality of time without quantity of time.

Suppose Joe Athlete went to his high school football coach with this proposal.

"Say, Coach. I'm going to be on your football team, you lucky guy. But I need for you to understand something right up front, Coach. I'm a busy high school senior. You know, girls and studying and girls. I can't give you a lot of practice time and I won't be able to make it to many of the team meetings, but here's what I'll do for you. I promise to be at practice every Thursday. And I guarantee it will be a quality practice."

Care to speculate on the coach's response? "Well, thanks so much, Joe. We really appreciate your making room for us in your schedule. We'll be looking forward to Thursdays!" NOT! More than likely, Joe would have been shown the door with the sound of "You're outta here!" still ringing in his ears as it slammed behind him. Why would we expect it to be any different in parenting? One of the ways kids spell love is T-I-M-E.

Up for a game of Jeopardy? The answer: *"Busyness."* The question? *"What is the greatest robber of time between parents and children?"* We've come to believe the myth that a good family is a busy family. A "good" family makes sure the kids are involved in all the right sports, taking all the right lessons, active in the right clubs, and . . . well, you get the point. In and of themselves, these things are not bad. But when taken to excess, they rob families of time together and leave little time for kids to be kids. Their impact on relationships? Barrenness rather than togetherness. If Satan can't make you a "bad" parent, the next best thing is to make you an overly "busy" parent . . . and the results will be about the same.

We parents often applaud our efforts at spending time with the family, giving ourselves "points" for being physically present in a room with our kids when, if the truth be known, we're in some other time warp, or behind a newspaper.

Perhaps you've had an experience similar to one Paul had on a Saturday morning at McDonald's. Vicky had an early-morning meeting at church, so Paul and Matthew went out for breakfast as they typically do on such occasions. Not particularly fond of McDonald's himself but acquiescing to his son's preference, Paul was mentally congratulating himself for being such a self-sacrificing dad, but his mind was a million miles away, thinking through his "To Do" list for the rest of the weekend. Matthew looked at Paul and said, "Dad, where are you?"

Kids need our time, but they also need our attention. They need parents who will enter their world and become involved at their level. Christ set the ultimate example. He left His world to enter ours, even though we didn't deserve it, to give us His attention, and ultimately to give His life.

Three aspects of time are of particular importance when it comes to parenting with intimacy. We would all do well to sear these into our brains. First, the time right now is important. During Matthew's infancy and early toddler years Paul was busy building his counseling practice. He was usually up and out of the house before Matthew was awake and home long after he was in bed. He assuaged his guilt by rationalizing that down the road he'd be able to spend more time with Matthew. After all, he was doing this in order to provide for Vicky and Matthew. This remains a source of great sadness for Paul because those years are irretrievable—and he missed them. *THE TIME NOW IS IMPORTANT.*

Second, all important things take time. What's the "take home" lesson? Don't judge the outcome by the score at halftime. If it's rough and difficult for you, don't predict the outcome by the score right now. Practice hope! *ALL IMPORTANT THINGS TAKE TIME.*

Third, take time to dream with your kids. It's your only bridge to the future. We're so reality-based and performance-oriented that we've forgotten how to dream. Dreaming with your kids is your only bridge to the future.

On Matthew's eighth birthday, he received a Texas Rangers shirt and a new glove. One afternoon a few days later Paul happened upon Matthew standing in front of the TV watching a Rangers game. Outfitted in his baseball pants, new shirt, cap, and glove, he was at the plate . . . bat in hand. Paul overheard him whispering to himself. "C'mon. Pitch it to me. I'm going to hit a home run to the right field seats." Visions of an ESPN post-game interview danced in his head.

Fortunately, Paul caught the words before they tumbled out of his mouth. He had almost jerked him back into reality with, "Matthew! What in the world are you doing? You know you're not supposed to have your bat in the house. And don't you have a bed to make and a room to clean? And, by the way, you do realize, don't you, that the chance of your ever making the Major Leagues is about one in a million!" Fortunately, on this particular Saturday afternoon, a little dreaming took place instead. "Hey, Matthew, hit one for me!" Father and son sat down and watched the game together, dreaming about what God could do with Matthew's life as a professional baseball player. *TAKE TIME TO DREAM WITH YOUR KIDS.*

Time is a precious commodity. Spend it wisely. As you invest it in your child, you're instilling a sense of identity that will reap benefits for eternity.

Instilling a Sense of Identity

This kind of investment in the life of a child sends a powerful message. "You belong in this family." It's impossible to overemphasize the importance of this message in instilling a sense of identity. People often ask, "Isn't the gang problem terrible! Why do kids get into gangs?" It's a complex answer, but the core problem is kids who join gangs don't feel like they belong to a family. They'll pay any price, including potentially their lives, to feel like they belong, to feel like they're "somebody."

Part of instilling a sense of identity involves letting your child know that it's OK to be a kid in this family. Kids don't exist in this family to make Mom and Dad feel or look good. It's OK to make mistakes. It's OK to misbehave every once in a while. Now, there will be consequences, but we expect you to act your age—not older, not younger. It's OK to be a kid.

Let's flash back a few years to the Warrens' garage. We'll let Paul tell you the story of . . .

The Case of Hitting the Nail on the Head

I've told this story many times, but I still feel sad every time I share it. It was Saturday morning . . . but this wasn't just any Saturday morning. This was Project Saturday. The project at hand was cleaning out the garage. I'd gotten a head start this particular morning. I'd already been to K-Mart and purchased one of those metal do-it-yourself shelves. I'm a card-carrying member of the Mechanically

Impaired Club, but I thought surely this was within my realm of competency.

By 10 A.M. I'm already frustrated. I've counted down twenty-seven holes from the top on each side, dutifully placed those crazy little cross bars in position that are supposed to provide stability, but the shelf was contorted and looked a little like the Leaning Tower of Pisa. My patience was growing thin, and I'm beginning to mutter (a nice euphemism!) to myself. Our dog, who was curled up a few feet away, cocked her head and looked worried.

About this time, my son Matthew, a first-grader at the time, came out into the garage. "Dad, I'm going to help you. I'm going to put this up." He held up one of those little plastic brackets that you use to hang brooms and the like. I'm on automatic pilot as I respond, "OK, Matthew, that's fine." Out of the corner of my eye I'm watching him but not really paying attention. I'm expecting him to be able to do an adult job. With one hand he's holding this plastic bracket up against the wall and with the other hand he's rearing back with an adult-sized hammer. As it comes forward. . . . "Whap!" He hit the nail square on the head . . . the first time. The next two times the hammer missed the designated target and smashed into the sheet-rock instead. Did I bother to help him out and teach him how to do this? Did I give him my attention? Did I meet his need? No way. I'm often "Joe Schmuck" when I'm not in my office. I make all the same mistakes that I talk to parents about.

"Matthew, just go inside! I guess you're not going to be able to do that!" Not only was I communicating in all exclamation points, but they were angry ones at that. I knew I'd blown it, and I felt terrible. But I didn't say anything . . . not then and not the rest of the afternoon or evening. A cloud seemed to hang over the house.

About 8:30 that evening, Matthew came into the study. "Goodnight, Dad."

"Goodnight, Matthew. Going to read a story with Mom?"

"Uh huh."

"OK. See you in the morning."

"Uh, Dad . . . "

"Yes, Matthew?"

"I enjoyed working with you in the garage this morning."

It felt like a dagger had gone into my chest, and I thought to myself, *Did your mom send you in here to say that?* even though I knew Vicky wouldn't do something like that. Before I could even respond, Matthew hit the nail squarely on the head.

"But, Dad, sometimes I think you want me to be a sixth-grader instead of a first-grader . . . and I just can't do that."

I'll never forget that night. I was painfully reminded that my son needed to know that it was OK to be six years old and that his dad loved him whether he hit the nail on the head or not.

The final piece to shaping your child's identity is helping him discover that he is more than the child of his earthly parents. Our children are on loan, entrusted to us by a Heavenly Father who loves them, cares for them, and has a plan for their lives. As parents we have the awesome responsibility—and privilege—of walking with them as they discover who God has created them to be and how He wants to involve them in impacting their world.

Ask Yourself

1. Take out a piece of paper and list each child's name. Next to each name list the child's hobbies or areas of interest. Now take out your calendar or appointment book and schedule play time with your children. Enter their world. Is your son interested in soccer, cars, baseball cards, Nintendo? Then find a place and a time when the two of you can play together. Let him teach you if your skill level or knowledge isn't up to par. Is your daughter interested in Girl Scouts, drill team, basketball, or art? Then enjoy these events together. Go with her to sell cookies, shoot baskets at the gym, or make chalk drawings on the sidewalk.

Does your child sense your interest in what's important to

her? Does she have memories of times when you have played together? Does she only have memories of doing things the adults thought were fun? Is the only time spent together in discipline, chores, or housework?

2. Carve out a few minutes with each child during the next few weeks and dream with her. What does she dream about? becoming a professional baseball player? going to Disneyland? finding a hidden treasure? Take off your adult "hat" and adult practicalities and just dream. Listen carefully and rediscover the joy of dreaming. Pretend with your child. You may discover things you never knew. What do their dreams communicate? Can you tell what's important to them? What dreams make them happy? Does anything make them afraid?

Experiencing Truth

Psalm 122:6 says, "May they prosper who love You." Make it a priority to provide security to each of your children. A child feels secure when he knows he belongs. Let your son or daughter know that he or she is an important part of your family. Here are some practical ideas:

* Make a special place for family photos and display individual as well as family snapshots.
* Take your child with you to the office one afternoon and show him the family mementos on your desk.
* Carve someone's initials on a tree in the backyard as a reminder of the family who lives there.
* Take turns fixing favorite meals — every family member gets to choose the dinner menu for Sunday nights.
* Encourage all family members to attend events that are important to individuals. It communicates a message of security when all siblings attend the grade schooler's choir performance — not just the parents.

Special Thoughts for Single Parents

Making a living and providing for your child is extremely important, but don't forget the little joys. You don't want to find yourself trying to provide food on the table and then not being around to eat it. Sometimes folding laundry can wait until after you've played with Barbie dolls. The laughter that comes from a giant tickle session in the middle of the living room floor is more valuable than a clean kitchen. Yes, you're busy; but it's the moments you steal away to have fun that make a relationship. Remember that kids don't exist in a family to make the parents feel good. Let your child know it's OK to be a kid. It is the little times that make such a big difference.

Special Thoughts for Blended Families

Playing with your children may look a little different in a blended family. You now have different ages, sexes, and preferences. Give yourself and your children permission to be sad if the family play times seem different. Grieve that loss. Then begin new traditions with your own family. Take into consideration the individual preferences. You might want to take turns choosing what the kids think would be fun to do together. You may want to establish the tradition of "Family Nights," where every member prioritizes time to have fun together. One child may want to spend time outdoors, and next week another may want to play table games. Give each family member an opportunity to voice his opinion and enjoy the support of family members.

Get rid of a "yours" and "mine" mentality. Your kids are your kids. Take every opportunity to celebrate the new family God has given you.

CHAPTER 7

Helping Your Child Identify Painful Emotions... An Open Door to Intimacy

EVEN THE MOST adventurous among us would have to agree that when facing uncharted territory our comfort level increases dramatically when the expertise of a tour guide is available. A "guided tour" implies that the one in a position of leadership has, indeed, been down this road before and knows the ins and outs, the "must sees" and "must dos" as well as the "danger zones." Imagine how disconcerting it would be if you were following your trusted guide faithfully down a narrow trail and innocently asked, "Where does this road lead?" only to hear this reply, "Don't know. Never been down this particular road before. Guess we'll find out together, won't we!"

The Warren family recently drove to San Antonio for a much-needed mini-vacation. On their way, they stopped at the Inner Space Caverns in Georgetown, Texas. They arrived just in time to join up with a group of approximately 100 energetic, eager, wide-eyed children from a local day care center. Rather than wait several hours to take a more "age-appropriate" tour, they decided to tag along with these little would-be explorers and their adult companions. What's the point? Hold on, we're getting there.

The tour guide had obviously done his homework and was extremely knowledgeable about the history of the caverns as well as the intricacies and distinguishing characteristics of each type of formation. The children were, of course, bubbling with curiosity; and he patiently and carefully answered each question. At one point, he leaned over to Paul and whispered, "Too bad you had to come today. If you were on another tour I'd be able to give you a lot more information and a lot more dates and stuff." That would've been nice, although Vicky felt quite satisfied with the level of explanation. You have to understand that Paul and Matthew are the scientific-types in the Warren household! What was impressive to Vicky was the fact that their guide was able to adapt his instruction to whatever level was needed. That's not an easy task!

As your child travels his as-yet-uncharted road toward maturity, he's looking to you as his tour guide, or journeymate. It may not be appropriate for you to tell him "everything" you know, especially if it would make things even scarier for him . . . tailor it to address what he needs for the moment. Ephesians offers some sound advice to parents. "Let no unwholesome word proceed from your mouth, but only such a word as is good for edification according to the need of the moment, that it may give grace to those who hear" (Eph. 4:29). This is perhaps nowhere more true than in the area of learning to deal with painful feelings.

Knock, Knock . . . Who's There?

Relax. This isn't another silly knock-knock joke. But it is about helping your child open the door to his or her emotions in order to identify what's on the other side. One of the things that sets us apart in God's creation is our language skills. In Genesis, one of Adam's assignments was to name the animals. Why was that? He could have just said, "Hey, you animals over there . . ." Could it have been, perhaps, so that he could have dominion over them? By being able to call each by name he established a more specific, individual relationship with each.

We would like to propose that until you can name your emotions, you'll never be able to have dominion over them. Kids are not born with the ability to name their feelings. This is part of your job as your child's journeymate. When an emotion can be called by its name it becomes less formidable as it is no longer part of that great sea of unknowns that face a growing child.

It's important for kids to be able to distinguish different types of emotions, otherwise there's a tendency for all emotions to go through what we like to call "The Anger Door." Kids often appear angry when a more painful emotion is actually lurking beneath the surface. Fear, sadness, and guilt are much more painful emotions than anger, so it's easier to express them through the anger door. It's important to help your children approach the anger door and ask the question, "Knock, Knock . . . Who's There?" and then be ready to help them deal with the answer.

"It's Fear."

All kids have fears (as do all adults, for that matter!). In fact, depending on the age of the child, those fears will be pretty predictable . . . fear of the dark, fear of monsters under the bed, fear of animals, etc. It's important for you as his journeymate to teach him how to handle these fears because when allowed to reign unchecked, fear is probably the most destructive of all emotions. Satan loves to use it as a tool to thwart the growing-up process. Most kids who manifest what we typically call "acting-out behaviors" are actually scared to death. It's never "cool" to admit to being scared, so he prefers to be perceived as hostile and Teflon-coated to cover up his fears.

So, how do you help your child handle his or her fears?

● *Help her identify it and give her permission to be afraid.* Be empathetic. "It looks to me like you might be feeling scared. You know, there's nothing wrong with being afraid. Everyone is fearful sometimes. I know I have been."

● *Balance his fears with the facts.* The key word here is *balance.* Saying things like, "That's the most ridiculous thing I ever heard of. You're too old to be afraid of that. Don't be a baby" is summarily unproductive and will slam the communication door as tight as a drum. Neither can you *make* his fears go away. You must acknowledge his fear and then help him look at the facts, remembering to be empathetic.

Consider this example. Most every child now has within her circle of friends at least one whose parents have divorced. Consequently, when a child hears his or her parents argue it stirs up fears that perhaps divorce could happen in her family as well. Balancing her fears with the facts would sound something like this.

"I know it might scare you when Dad and I disagree. In case you're ever worried that we might get a divorce, I want you to know that we're committed to staying together. Even though we don't always agree about everything and sometimes get upset with each other, we love each other very much and are committed to healing our hurts and always being there for you."

Or, if a child is afraid of thunderstorms, balancing fear with facts might sound like, "I know you're afraid of the storm. It sounds really mean, doesn't it. Kind of like somebody up in the sky is really mad. But that's just the noise the storm makes. Nobody's mad, and the weatherman said the storm should only last about another hour. Your mom and I are here with you, and we're not going to let anything bad happen to you. Would you like to read one of your favorite stories to take your mind off the storm?" (For younger children, if there is a persistent source of fear, you might try to find a story about the subject to read at times when the fear resurfaces.)

• *"Follow Jesus' example."* The next step is to let them know through words as well as actions that you will be with them. When they're little children, that means that in a literal, physical sense you'll be with them. You'll help them get through it. As they get older, this takes on a more symbolic form. Aside from the promise of eternal life, one of the most precious promises in all of Scripture is, "Lo, I am with you always" (Matt. 28:20). As Christ's earthly ambassador to your children, you have an opportunity to give that same comfort to them by assuring them that you will walk through this scary situation with them. Notice, we said "with" them.

It's not saying, "Oh, you poor baby. This is too scary for you. Let me handle this for you." On the other extreme, it's not, "Yep, it's pretty scary all right. Hope you get through this OK. See you on the other side." It's getting in the middle. "I can understand you're scared. But let's look at the situation and see how you can handle it. I'm going to walk through this with you, and I know together we can face it." As you walk hand-in-hand with him, for the younger child perhaps literally and as he grows older symbolically, he will draw strength from your love and support . . . just as we do from Christ's. Scripture reminds us, "There is no fear in love; but perfect love casts out fear" (1 John 4:18).

It's imperative that we address one other fear-related issue before answering the next knock on the door, and that's the issue of parents making decisions based on fear. This is perhaps the most destructive force warring against healthy parenting today. Fear immobilizes parents and renders them ineffective. The best parenting verse in the entire Scriptures is not really a parenting verse per se. Nevertheless, it offers three powerful parenting tools. It's found in 2 Timothy 1:7, "For God has not given us a spirit of timidity [fear], but of power and love and discipline [sound judgment]."

Power—the God-given authority given to us as parents.

Love—the kind that says, "I'm committed to doing whatever is truly in your best interest."

Sound Judgment—Ask God for wisdom and then use your head, your God-given common sense, and parental instincts to follow His leading.

"It's Sadness."

No one is exempt from sadness, not even Jesus. We often joke about John 10:35 being the verse of choice when it comes to Scripture memorization because it's the shortest verse in the entire Bible—"Jesus wept." But it's actually quite profound. Jesus felt great sadness at the death of His friend, Lazarus, particularly as He saw the sadness of Mary.

Sadness is perhaps the most painful of all emotions.

Therefore, it's easy to see why, as we've already discussed, it frequently turns to anger. Sadness will inevitably be experienced. It is part and parcel of growing up because there's a sense of loss as a child moves from one phase to another. With the excitement of all new things gained, there is the accompanying sadness over things lost and left behind.

Just a note of distinction, childhood depression is not the same as sadness. A combination of sadness, anger, and anxiety, childhood depression endures over a longer period of time and is more debilitating. Experiences of sadness are an essential and unavoidable part of growing up, but depression should be seen as a problem and treatment sought. Depression can result from a child not experiencing the freedom to express anger, sadness, or anxiety.

The inevitable hurts, shuns, and cruelties of life press in on children just as surely as they do adults. Learning to deal with the companions of sadness and grief is an essential part of growing up, and yet children are seldom taught how to be sad. Adults tend to be uncomfortable with their own sadness, not to mention that of their children. Consequently, a sense of aloneness is added to the child's already-existing sadness.

Some common questions children ask hint at the loneliness of sadness.

- *"Does anybody know that I feel sad?"*
- *"Does anyone else feel sad?"*
- *"Will I feel sad forever?"*

These questions need to be answered. However, many times parents are caught up in giving correction, advice, facts, or trying to make the sadness go away. The greater need is for comfort. Matthew 5:4 was written for children as well as adults. "Blessed are those who mourn, for they shall be comforted." As a child experiences comfort at the point of their sadness, blessing comes as aloneness subsides. This removal of "aloneness" may be one of the most significant ingredients in parenting with intimacy.

Comforting a child in her sadness involves several steps. Each is vitally important and must be followed in an orderly sequence.

Children must be given permission to be sad. It's not a child's job to be "strong" so adults can lean on him for strength or to cover up his sadness so as to make life more convenient and hassle-free for adults. He must be allowed to cry and to talk about his sadness.

Let them know you feel sad for them because you love them and care for them. Don't dismiss the importance of this step, assuming they already know that. They need to hear it. They don't need advice or correction. They need comfort; and we give comfort through our presence as well as our God-given gift of language. "I feel sad for you. I feel sad to see you hurting. I want you to know I love you and am here for you." These are words that build up and minister grace (Eph. 4:29).

Share a bit of yourself with them. Share with them times when you've felt sad. Be sensitive so as not to make it sound as though you're dismissing their sadness as being unimportant. The goal is not to communicate, "You think you've got it bad. That's nothing. Why, when I was your age, I had something happen that was REALLY sad." The goal of self-disclosure is to let them see you as a real person with real emotions who can empathize with how they're feeling.

Offer them some realistic hope. Acknowledge that the sadness is painful now but that better times will come and that sharing their sadness will help it heal. An important measure of this hope comes from your self-disclosure. It gives reassurance that even though great sadness is experienced one can still experience the blessing of comfort and move on with life, strengthened in one's faith.

It's imperative to go in this order. Don't start telling them why they should be hopeful. First you must enter their world and minister to their aloneness.

"It's Guilt."

In the field of mental health, guilt has gotten a bad name. The early years of psychiatry taught that guilt was the worst thing ever foisted upon mankind by religion—an idea propagated and nurtured by, among others, Sigmund Freud himself. Of course, some on the religious end of the spectrum had an answer to that: "It's the only way you can motivate some people to do anything!"

There are two kinds of guilt. True guilt comes by way of the Spirit's conviction (John 16:8) as a result of breaking God's righteous laws and is based in our relationship with God the Heavenly Father. True guilt always offers the opportunity for restitution and restoration of the relationship through confession and forgiveness. First John 1:9 promises that "If we confess our sins, He is faithful and righteous to forgive us our sins and to cleanse us from all unrighteousness." The purpose of true guilt is always to lead back to restoration of the relationship through confession and forgiveness—whether between us and God or between parents and children.

False guilt is really not guilt or "conviction" at all. Rather, it's actually "condemnation" as it includes some of Satan's favorite emotional tools—fear plus self-directed anger. (Check out the good news found in Rom. 8:1.) The rampant fear is based not in our relationship with God but in our relationship with other people. False guilt includes the fear that one could do something to lose the love of somebody they cherish. The self-directed anger comes from the child's orientation that "If something bad has happened, it must be my fault." Both are absolutely destructive as they rob a child of the energy necessary to grow up. Because we live in a fallen world—fallen physically, emotionally, and spiritually—all kids experience false guilt, Satan's counterfeit. All kids struggle with false guilt as they're learning about trust. One of the beautiful things about healthy discipline is it teaches kids that false guilt is unnecessary. They learn that if they make a mistake there are consequences, but with their parent's guidance they can face those consequences and move on. They discover that their parents never stop loving them. They loved them before, during, and after the mistake. Healthy discipline is such a vital tool in helping children resolve this issue, we will be devoting the entire next chapter to it. Self-directed anger that says "Everything's my fault" is displaced through parents who admit their own faults through confession and repentance—experiencing a renewed focus on meeting the child's intimacy needs.

Remember, true guilt offers an opportunity for restoration—false guilt does not.

"It's Anger."

Suppose anger answers the door—this time not masked as some other emotion. Is it OK to be angry? For a child to be angry? For *your* child to be angry? We've probably all said it or had it said to us as a child. "Don't you be angry with me, young man (young woman)! You wipe that angry look off your face!"

There's a saying that goes like this: All emotions are acceptable; all behaviors are not. Anger has gotten a pretty bad rap because it's often manifest by some pretty unacceptable behaviors. Ephesians 4:26-27 acknowledges that we will be angry at times but also addresses the appropriate manifestation of our anger. "Be angry, and yet do not sin; do not let the sun go down on your anger, and do not give the devil an opportunity." Backing up one more verse to verse 25, you'll notice it begins with the word *"Therefore."*

Many of us have been taught to always ask the question, "What's that *therefore* there for?" It's there to point us to the preceding twenty-four verses that talk about living in harmony, maintaining unity, not giving in to the old lusts of the flesh, practicing humility, gentleness, patience, forbearance, speaking the truth in love . . . need we go on? So that *therefore* is there for the purpose of setting some guidelines as to how we are to relate to one another so that when anger does surface it can be resolved without the devil being given any opportunity to stick his mangy head through the door.

How can you help your children be angry and sin not? This is going to sound repetitious, but the first step is:

Help them identify the feeling.   A young child does not have the language skills to sit down and tell you, "You know, Dad (or Mom), I'm really angry. I noticed that my adrenalin is rising, and I feel this anger welling up inside me. I'd like to talk through the causes and sources of my anger with you and see if we can't come to some sort of healthy resolution because I know that otherwise I will suffer painful emotional consequences."

Remember what we've said. If you can't name it, you'll have difficulty controlling it. So the first step is helping your child to give their feeling a name.

"Boy, you look angry! I can tell you're really mad!"

Give them permission to be angry.   You're not giving them permission to be disrespectful or destructive, but you're giving them permission to feel what they're feeling without compelling them to get rid of it. Remind them that all emotions are acceptable, but all behaviors are not.

Help them learn how to appropriately deal with their anger.   At this juncture, let's look for a few moments at something we affectionately refer to as "The Teapot Principle."

Imagine, if you will, Tim Teapot sitting on the burner. He's full of water, and as the fire is turned up he soon reaches the boiling point. As the water begins to churn, what happens? Eventually, Tim will begin to spout and make that shrill, annoying noise that teapots make. (Which are actually signals for help and cries for attention.) What are our choices?

We could stand in front of Tim Teapot and say, "I just love to hear you spout, Timmy. It's so good to hear you actualize yourself. Go ahead and boil and spit. Just spout away." What's going to happen? Timmy's going to burn out. Can a charred, burned out teapot ever be repaired or fully restored?

"Of course not! We knew that! Kids are to be seen and not heard. Anybody knows that what you need to do is go to the local hardware store, buy the biggest cork you can find, and stuff it in Tim's spout. That'll teach him to spout off in front of us! He'll think twice before he does that again!"

What will happen to Tim? Your first response is probably that he'll explode as the pressure builds up. Or, he may become incredibly depressed. Or, and this is actually a combination of the first two (and a deadly combination at that), he'll become bitter. Bitterness is simply unresolved anger that's been repeatedly stuffed. Hebrews 12:15 tells us not to let a root of bitterness grow up among us lest it defile us. What does *defile* mean? Ruin. Spoil. Render ineffective.

If you could take your brain out and look at it (don't try this at home!), you would discover that the anger center, the rage center, lives right next door to a portion of the language center and the sexuality center. Do not let anger remain stuffed and unresolved. Do not let bitterness grow up among you lest your language and sexuality centers be defiled. It's interesting to note that the crime of rape is not a sexual crime primarily. It's a crime of anger. It's no accident that in our culture one of the most common ways to express anger at someone is a four-letter word that is slang for human intercourse. Do not let a root of bitterness, unresolved anger, grow up amongst you lest you become defiled.

OK, so if we don't let them boil and we don't cork their anger, what are we to do? Teaching our children how to be angry is every bit as important, probably more so, than teaching them to do schoolwork, how to brush their teeth, how to ride a bike, how to manage their allowance, or how to cross a busy street.

Tim Teapot needs to learn how to assertively use the energy in his anger. It may be necessary at first to remove him from the fire. Tim needs time to cool off. Call this time-out, a cooling off period, whatever. Then Tim needs to learn how to take the energy inherent in his anger and use it to address the underlying issues. Through words and actions the steam is taken and used to extinguish the flame that is causing the anger.

Using your God-given gift of language, talk through

with your children what's making them angry. Help them look "underneath" the anger for other emotions like hurt that needs comfort or fear that needs reassurance. Help them identify intimacy needs that may be going unmet and teach them how to express them: "I'm getting frustrated with my homework and think I need some help." "Our bedtime rules seem unfair; can we talk?" Parents can encourage this learning process even from the earliest ages: "Sammy, when you get fussy like you are now, I wonder if you're needing a hug? Come let me hold you and tell you a story." "Aaron, your anger makes me wonder if something happened today at school that we need to visit about? I'd sure like to." These "gentle answers" from parents help turn away wrath (Prov. 15:1)—and help get to the real issues and intimacy needs.

It's important also to teach your child how to pray and ask God how to be angry. Sound strange? Doesn't God tell us to pray about everything? "Everything" is certainly inclusive of learning to manage one's anger appropriately.

"Dear God, thank You for this dinner. Thank You for our warm house. Thank You for helping me with my history test. And, God, could You help me learn how to be angry in the right way." Music to God's ears!

Ministering to Your Child's Aloneness

Feelings such as we've described in this chapter—fear, sadness, guilt, anger—can be overwhelming for a child. And sometimes when we feel overwhelmed, we also feel alone. Remember how God ministered to Adam's aloneness? He gave him Eve. He has given your children—you! God wants to minister to your child's aloneness through you. This is not to say that they won't need times to be alone, but we don't learn in isolation.

Respond to your child with what you can do—not what you can't change. Yes, it's a cruel world and in many respects you can't change that. But you can provide a safe haven, a protected environment for them in which emotions can be safely shared. Every child will experience hurt in life. Your job as parents is not to provide black-and-white rules in order to straighten them out. That's important, but not sufficient. Every child needs a mom and a dad who will be there to help heal the inevitable hurts so they don't fester into boils of shame, rage, paralyzing fear, or consuming false guilt. As you do so, you'll also be pointing them beyond yourself—to the God of all comfort and a God who is love!

"Son or Daughter, I know life can be tough. But I want you to know I'm here to help you discover your feelings. Let's find a way to use them to build relationships instead of destroying them." Every day seek to be a healer in the lives of your children.

Let no unwholesome word proceed from your mouth, but only
such a word as is good for edification according to the
need of the moment, that it may give grace to those who hear.
Ephesians 4:29

Ask Yourself

1. All children experience the unpleasant emotions of anger, fear, sadness, and guilt. Are you communicating to your child that all emotions are appropriate, but all behaviors are not? How do you deal with your own unpleasant emotions? Is it OK to be angry in your family? How are feelings of sadness handled in your household? How do you respond to your child's feelings of true guilt, false guilt/condemnation?

2. Do you avoid the extremes of managing fear? Are you giving your child the message that she can't handle facing the fears? Or are you giving the message that it's not OK to be afraid? Have you heard yourself saying, "Don't be silly. There's nothing to be afraid of. . ."?

3. Do you avoid the extremes of managing anger? Do you insist that the child "stuff" his anger, or do you let the child rage without any intervention? Have you begun to teach your child how to be angry? Does he know how to express his feelings and needs with words instead of using actions?

Experiencing Truth

Proverbs 15:1 says, "A gentle answer turns away wrath [anger], but a harsh word stirs up anger." Many times the response of anger is a direct result of an emotional need going unmet. For example, you may be needing affection and reach out to hold your partner's hand. If he pulls away, your need for affection has just gone unmet. You, in turn, may respond with anger. Similarly, your child may need acceptance from a friend, but receive rejection instead. Your child may express anger as a result of the rejection—perhaps toward the friend, a sibling, or you.

Look sensitively at any outbursts of anger this week. Try to discern if an unmet need may have provoked the anger. Most of all, resist reacting with your own harsh words. Let your gentle answer turn away wrath. For example:

A child who needs big doses of security may respond in anger if left in the nursery or day care. Let your words speak gently to her need. *I know you're going to miss Mommy while I'm in my class, and I will miss you too. Miss Karen will be here with you. I'll see you after snack time.*

Special Thoughts for Single Parents

If you haven't finished dealing with your own emotional pain, there will be a greater tendency for you to respond unproductively to your children. You will be more likely to blame, criticize, minimize, or give logic in response to their emotion. (You may want to refer back to the section on "Emotional Responding" in chap. 4.) Remember, the worst way to have to deal with feelings is to deal with them alone. Find a journeymate for yourself, and then be a journeymate for your child.

It may be a particular challenge for you to know how to deal with a child's disappointments because of an ex-spouse's behavior. Avoid blaming or criticizing your ex-spouse. But also avoid "sugarcoating" the issue. Your child needs adults who will face the truth with him—sometimes people do things that hurt us.

Then he needs adults who give comfort for that hurt. "It saddens me that you were hurt this weekend because I care about you. I love you, and it hurts me that you were hurt."

Special Thoughts for Blended Families

As a stepparent, how do you respond when a child misses his biological parent? Do you feel threatened? jealous? or compassionate? Your child needs permission to talk about missing the other parent. She needs to be provided with an environment that is safe enough to express those emotions. Your child also needs to know that she can rely on you to take responsibility for what you can control—your own responses. Your child may experience two very different emotional climates when she moves from one household to another. Importantly, we first provide a safe and secure emotional place of "refuge" in our home. Second, even though you can't control the other environment, you can be empathetic of pain that may be experienced there.

CHAPTER 8

Children As Your
Dearest Disciples

DONALD HAD STRUGGLED throughout his ministry with being a workaholic. He and his wife were together on that label. No disagreement there. Fourteen, sixteen hours a day sometimes. He was always at the church or visiting church members. He had tried to change, even shedding tears on many occasions over his compulsion to work. One day, with tears running down his cheeks, he asked David, "David, why? Why won't I go home? I have children who need me. Why won't I go home?"

As they talked, he began to pour out his heart. Toward the end of their time together, he said, "You know, I think a major reason why I don't go home is I'm afraid. I'm afraid that I don't know how to be a father. I know my children need me, but I'm not sure I know what they need. I'm not sure I know how to give it to them. I feel adequate here at the church, in my ministry. I feel adequate preaching, managing, discipling my congregation. But I don't feel adequate with my own children."

So, Donald invested himself, sometimes to the point of exhaustion, in discipling his congregation, while his dearest disciples, his own children, waited for their father to come home. Donald's not alone. He represents many parents—fathers and mothers alike from many walks of life—who, feeling inadequate with their own children, direct their energies toward building into the lives of others first, feeding the "leftovers" to those at home.

The Greek word for "disciple" simply means a "learner,

one who is taught, a follower." It was Christ's goal that He impart His very life to His disciples. With this as His goal, He shared His conflicts, His joys, His prayer life, and His relationship with the Father. He thus became the "context" or setting for His own teaching. This is what discipleship is all about—as Paul shares with the Thessalonians—imparting *"not only the gospel of God but also our own lives" (1 Thes. 2:8).*

Jesus Christ stands without comparison in a multitude of ways. Among them is His uniqueness in propagating His message. Other so-called "religious leaders" might establish great schools or generate voluminous writings—but not Jesus! He simply trained disciples! He did not build great monuments, structures, or libraries—but transformed lives. This is still the secret of truly propagating the Gospel—as men and women become disciples of Christ and then are used by God to challenge others in discipleship. The essence of Christ's call to making disciples is found in this proverb: "I may impress people from a distance but I can only impact them up close!" Thus, parents are called to impart their very lives to their children and, by doing so, impact them positively for Christ. This matter of true discipleship lies at the very heart of "success" in the Christian home. "Disciplining" a child is done a great injustice when we remove it from this larger framework of discipleship.

Mothers often lament having to put their desires to be involved in a discipleship ministry on a back burner until their children are at least old enough to be in school all day. Fathers often look to the workplace or within the church for men to disciple, as Donald did. What if fathers and mothers in "training up their children in the way they should go" saw as their priority the "discipling" of their own children—modeling for them a life of Christlikeness and then spending the time and love necessary to see this Christlikeness reproduced in their children? After all, how difficult is it to lead a consistent Christlike life in front of someone you meet with once a week for an hour? In contrast, the challenge to live out your faith twenty-four hours a day in front of your children is one guaranteed to keep your feet to the fire. This is the essence of parenting with intimacy!

Ingredients for "Disciplining" Your Children

Discipline is simply defined as teaching your children to be responsible for themselves. Or, we might think of it as a form of pain management—a little pain now to avoid a lot of pain later! Although it doesn't "feel" like it to the child at times, healthy discipline is the parents' expression of their unconditional love. It represents their willingness to do whatever is in the best interest of their child, even though it will more than likely not be received as such.

Have you ever had this experience? You're sitting at the breakfast table enjoying that first cup of coffee and reading the newspaper. Your daughter (or son) sits down next to you, excitedly pulls the paper from your hands and gushes, "Dad, I just want to tell you . . . thanks so much for grounding me last night. I realize that I am self-centered, materialistic, and narcissistic; and that you were only doing what was in my best interest when you refused to let me buy everything I wanted at the mall. You and Mom are doing a great job with me. I'm so lucky to have you as parents!" You're still waiting, aren't you? But don't we kind of wait for our kids to give us that kind of feedback and then get offended when they don't? Unconditional love says, "I'm committed to doing whatever is in your best interests, whether you agree with me or not." Let's look at several key ingredients that are included into this process of disciplining, i.e., discipling, your children.

(1) Intimacy—Establishing closeness is the fundamental ingredient in disciplining your child. Just as surely as bread without yeast will never rise, trying to discipline a child in an environment lacking intimacy will be disastrous. There must be a foundation of love and friendship and a proper balance of love and discipline. It's those whom the Lord loves that He then disciplines (Heb. 12:6). He provides intimate love first, then discipline.

It's quite possible that you may have been hurt and scarred because that balance was improper as you were growing up. In many homes, the philosophy of discipline goes something like this. "You *(mother)* give them the love;

I'll *(father)* give them the discipline." Wrong! Do not pass Go. Do not collect $200. Love and discipline must fit together like a hand fits in a glove. Each parent must be involved in both. The child must see that the same hand that disciplines them also loves and comforts them.

When discipline is administered in an atmosphere in which there is no intimacy or too little intimacy, the child will grow up to resent the discipline (and the discipliner) and a root of bitterness will begin to grow. The child ends up with a mind-set that says, "There is this stranger who seems to enter my life at the point when I'm doing something wrong and inflicts punishment on me, and I resent that." There's possibly no quicker way to "provoke a child to anger" (Eph. 6:4) than to discipline without intimacy.

Intimacy takes time. In contrast, you can quickly spank a child or send her to her room. Developing intimacy with your child requires an investment of time; but the yield on your investment will be higher than any interest-bearing account you could ever hope to open.

(2) Instruction—Children need to be told what needs to be done. This too takes time. Parents need to sit down with their children and explain what they want them to do. Whenever possible, express your expectations in a positive form. For example, "Please take your clothes to the laundry room" will be more effective than "Quit leaving your clothes thrown everywhere!"

Also, don't expect them to read your mind. Rules and expectations must be clear and consistent. Help them understand the "big picture"—that the goal is not just compliance on their part but helping them learn to be responsible for themselves. Focus on the positive. A special word of caution to dads is warranted at this juncture. Be careful what expectations you convey to your children. Too often, statements like this one are made by frustrated parents: "If you can't straighten yourself out, you're never going to amount to anything," or "Can't you do anything right?" It's eerie how often these "prophetic" statements come to fruition. Instead, instill confidence by saying things like, "Your mom and I know you can handle this." Reassure them that you'll be nearby and that they can always come back to home plate for a visit with the umpires!

(3) Training (in how to do it) — All parents will agree (especially dads!) that the three most dreaded words on Christmas Eve are "Some Assembly Required." As you sit down with the box, you tip it upside down, dumping all 355 parts on the floor, and proceed to correctly put each piece in the proper place with no instructions — right? Hardly. Why, even with the instruction manual, it often requires several attempts before some semblance of victory can be claimed. Why, then, would we expect our children to know not only *what* they should do but *how* they should do it without help?

This calls to mind the proverb that says, "Buy a man a fish, feed him for a day. Teach a man to fish, feed him for a lifetime." The best training is through your example! How you talk respectfully, how you help around the house, how you remain gentle when provoked. Many chores require hands-on training. For example, "Take out the trash" may sound simple to you but not to an eight-year-old. It often includes everything from (1) find all the small trash containers — hidden around the house; (2) empty them; (3) replace trash liners; (4) return trash containers to their previous locations. Show them how, then do it together, then turn them loose!

(4) Warning (the consequences): "You can ride your bike when your homework is finished." "You can borrow the car after the lawn is mowed." "We can keep playing with the blocks if you don't throw them." Be specific and positive. Have a repertoire of consequences that are age-appropriate and "fit the crime," keeping in mind that the consequences are always in the best interest of the child, not the parent.

Some situations may be dealt with simply with words of correction and a call to accountability. At other times, you'll want to guide your child into seeing the natural and logical consequences of her actions. For example, "It's your choice whether you do your homework or not; but if you choose not to you must realize that you'll get a "0" on that assignment which will affect your grade in that class. And if you don't pass the class, you won't be able to play volleyball" (Natural Consequence). Or, "If you choose not to do your chores, you won't be able to go out with your friends Saturday night" (Logical Consequence). Perhaps the most difficult (and humbling) of all consequences is having to make at least partial restitution for one's actions. For example, "If you wear your sister's nail polish again without her permission, you will have to buy her a new bottle from your allowance."

It's at this stage that you have the opportunity to teach your child about the importance of developing daily discipline. How many times have you heard these words from your child? "Why do I have to make my bed? I'm just going to get back into it tonight?" If simply making the bed was the only issue, that would make a lot of sense. However, the higher goal is developing discipline.

David and Eric took a few spins around that, "Why do I have to make my bed?" merry-go-round. During one of those spins, David remembered a similar conversation he had had with Teresa just a few months earlier.

"Honey, why do I have to keep putting up all this junk in the bathroom every day after I use it? I'm just going to turn around and get it right back out tomorrow morning."

David was dealing with a childhood issue of discipline that he had never learned as a child. His mother had followed him around and picked up after him constantly.

Over lunch one day, David asked Teresa, "Honey, what are some things I'm doing that irritate you?"

"I'm glad you asked! Sometimes I think I'm supposed to follow you around and pick up after you. I end up feeling unappreciated."

She got David's attention, and things began to change. On Eric and David's next spin around the "Why do I have to . . ." merry-go-round, David pointed out to Eric that the issue really wasn't making the bed—or picking up the bathroom countertop. The issue was the daily discipline of doing what's needed . . . or experiencing the consequences. No make bed. No ride bike. No pickup bathroom.

No happy wife.

In the Bible it's called the law of the harvest. "Whatsoever a man sows, that he also reaps." This is an important lesson for a child to learn; and, as David's example shows, if not learned as a child, it follows us into adulthood!

(5) Correction (implement consequences) — Correction *(discipline)* is based on what the child has been warned is going to happen. Not capricious or arbitrary, it's already been well thought out — discussed and agreed upon by Mom and Dad and communicated to the child. No surprises. If you just start pulling consequences out of the air for whatever seems to be the need of the moment, you'll end up with inconsistency, and sometimes irrationality if anger enters the picture. Then, feeling guilty for having overreacted, you won't follow through. This results, interestingly enough, in your child feeling insecure, living in an inconsistent environment in which he or she doesn't know what to expect next.

It's important to distinguish between discipline and punishment. The goal of discipline, or correction, is to help the child become responsible, to teach self-control. The goal of punishment, on the other hand, is to extract retribution or inflict a penalty. It's possible to "punish" anyone who's smaller than you are. That's what empowers bullies to impose themselves on their "victims." Discipline, however, has a much higher degree of accountability and purpose. You can only discipline someone you know, someone whose world you've entered for the purpose of developing an intimate relationship. Proverbs 3:12 speaks powerfully to this. "For whom the Lord loves He reproves, even as a father the son *in whom he delights.*"

An important key to maintaining this balance between love and discipline is to never withhold intimacy needs as a type of consequence. At times you will withhold privileges, toys, play times, and keys to the car — but not affection, comfort, acceptance, and security.

(6) Reassure — As parents maintain loving intimacy through continuing to meet their child's intimacy needs, the child's identity is positively shaped as their "worth" is

A Parenting Tip:
Discipline... Don't Punish

	Punishment	Discipline
Purpose	Retribution and penalty	To train and mature
Attitude	Parental frustration, hostility, or rejection	Parental concern with love
Emphasis	Past wrongs	Future—improved behavior and attitude
Child's Emotional Response	Anger Condemnation Fear	Security and gratitude; Positive sense of worth
Child's Concept of God	God seeks to punish and is therefore to be avoided	God loves and protects through discipline; He is available and worth knowing intimately

affirmed and separated from their "behavior." This will help prepare them to relate intimately to God who at the very same time "demonstrates His own love toward us, in that while we were yet sinners, Christ died for us" (Rom. 5:8). Without this clear separation, a child is held captive to the lie that her worth equals her behavior or performance.

Through touch, words, hugs, and other expressions of love, communicate acceptance and worth as affection, affirmation, and encouragement are given. What you're communicating to the child at this point is, "I'm displeased with your behavior, but I'm separating your behavior from your worth as a person. I am committed to you and love you unconditionally. There's nothing you could ever do that would make me stop loving you."

How many of us go through life afraid that we could do something to lose the love of someone we care about? And, if we're honest, we would have to admit that much of what we do in life is based on a drivenness to perform for God because we're afraid we could do something to lose His love. Attention, parents! You have an opportunity right here to lay the foundation for a life motivated from an attitude of gratitude rather than fear. Don't pass it up. You can give your children a gift that will last a lifetime. Give them the security of knowing that no matter what they *do* you will always love them. And, as they filter their concept of God, their Heavenly Father, through the lens of how they see their earthly parents, the groundwork has been laid. They are able to live lives resting securely in the arms of a God who loves them with a love that is perfect and complete. It is this "perfect love" that casts out fear (1 John 4:18-19). Do not minimize the impact of this step of reassurance. Your children will reap what you sow—now and for generations to come.

Why Children Misbehave ... Look for the Needs Beneath the Deeds

In explaining misbehavior, parents sometimes describe their children as "rotten," "spoiled," "bad," or "little monsters."

These labels roll easily off the tongue in times of parental frustration. Rather than see behavior changes, such labeling often results in a child feeling resentful and discouraged. It's true that children, just like their parents, will act-out as testimony of their "fallenness"—their lack of relating intimately with their Creator. But, in large part, children tend to misbehave when they feel discouraged or hurt in some way, and they engage in misguided efforts in an attempt to have their intimacy needs met.

Your child needs your investment of time in trying to discern the reasons behind their misbehavior. It's very easy to walk in on a child, see his acting-out behavior, and discipline him based only on what appears on the surface. That seldom tells the story, however. Realizing that your time's in short supply, we must implore you once again, however, to spend it wisely. No other pull on your time could be of greater importance than trying to discern the need beneath your child's deed. It is best to *look beyond* the misbehavior and try to understand what he is feeling. With an understanding of the feelings which led to misbehavior, you'll be able to guide and discipline him in the most effective and appropriate way.

To aid you as you embark on this discovery process, it might be helpful to know that there are three major issues that may lead your child to feel discouraged to the point that she resorts to misbehavior:

Need for Attention

All children have a need for attention. They try very hard to win attention by pleasing their parents. However, if they don't receive adequate attention in this way, they may resort to getting attention by irritating their parents. In a child's mind, it's better to get attention for bad behavior than to be *ignored*.

If your child's misbehavior leaves you feeling annoyed, and you find yourself repeatedly asking him to behave, maybe he's sending an attention S.O.S. A child may stop misbehaving temporarily, after you ask him to stop, but later do the same kind of thing. This may also suggest the need for attention.

The best way to respond is to begin paying more attention to good behavior while ignoring her annoying behavior. Think of ways to give her more positive attention, i.e., schedule some fun family nights or spend some quality time with just this one child.

Need to Feel More Secure

It's discouraging for a child to feel powerless and insecure. Sometimes a child tries to assert himself by saying things like, "You can't make me," or "I will if I want to." When a child acts this way, the parent tends to feel angry and threatened. If the parent tries to win the argument, the child may continue to be defiant or may obey the parent in a provoking, deviant way.

The best way to handle a power struggle with your child is to back off, stay calm, and encourage her to cooperate with you. Fighting with a child only increases the need for power—it solves nothing! A helpful approach is to respond with gentle reassurance. *"A gentle answer turns away wrath, but a harsh word stirs up anger"* (Prov. 15:1).

This would be a perfect place for a little pop quiz. Ready? Answer these questions with a "Yes" or "No."

___ I can control the thoughts inside my child's head.
___ I can control the words that come out of my child's mouth.
___ I can control my child's behavior.
___ I can control my child's attitude.
___ I can control the look on my child's face.

If you answered no to all five, you made a perfect score—and are wise. Although every parent has *tried* to control one or all of these, it's not possible. "Well, gosh. If you can't control the thoughts in their heads, the words that come out of their mouths, their behavior, their attitudes, or the looks on their faces—what's a parent to do!"

Don't give up yet. There are two powerful areas over which you are in full control—(1) your response and (2) the consequences. Choose not to get involved in the inevitable power struggles in which they'll try to engage you. Stand firm in the two areas that are under your jurisdiction.

By your refusing to take the responsibility for controlling their thoughts, words, behavior, their attitude, or what's on their face, guess who that leaves it with? Right. The ball's back in their court. As you administer the consequence, a child is challenged with his responsibility to do the right thing with the ball! Remember, the goal of discipline is teaching him to be responsible for himself. And part of teaching him responsibility involves allowing him to fail while it's still safe to fail.

Unresolved Hurt/Anger

Sometimes children feel so discouraged and hurt that they doubt that others love them. When this happens, they may hurt others as they feel they have been hurt. Parents should be aware that they aren't necessarily the "cause" of this kind of behavior . . . the hurt may have come from a friend or classmate. But home is often the safest place to vent the hurt.

Avoid criticism, punishment, or getting even. An attempt to "battle it out" may eventually lead the child to feel very hopeless and unlovable. It's best to respond by showing love. If it is suspected that there is unresolved hurt/anger toward the parent it will be important to "heal" this hurt through sharing, understanding, empathizing, and oftentimes confession and forgiveness. If the hurt/anger is related to someone else, but is being dumped or "displaced" on the parent, the parent needs to respond with calm reassurance and avoid "personalizing" the hurtful words. After reassuring empathy has prompted calmness, discussion of the "real" hurt can be undertaken. Later, instructing and training the child in "speaking the truth in love" (Eph. 4:15) may be helpful in reducing "displaced" anger.

Although parents don't cause children to misbehave, problems can become worse if parents don't seek to understand their child's needs and feelings and respond as *adults!* As parents respond to the needs of a child, they role model Christ's love and point the child toward the "God who supplies all your needs" (see Phil. 4:19)—preparing them to one day consider the eternal significance of needing to relate intimately not only to parents but also to their Creator through His Son Jesus Christ. Once again, the opportunity affords itself to respond as Jesus would.

Jesus Looked Beyond Our Faults and Saw Our Needs

On many occasions in the New Testament, Jesus looked beyond an individual's fault (their misdeeds) and looked straight into his heart at his needs. One example jumps readily to mind—Zaccheus, the tax collector. When we catch up with Zaccheus in Luke 19, what has he been doing? He had been stealing from his countrymen. Odds are good that he was also lying, cheating, and deceiving people. He hears Jesus is coming to town so he climbs up in a sycamore tree to get a better view (since he was a short little guy). What are we told about Jesus' encounter with Zaccheus? Jesus stopped and looked up into the tree. It's important to note what Jesus *did not* do. He didn't look up at Zaccheus and say, "You lying, cheating thief! Come down from there and stop it!" Even though Jesus knew all about Zaccheus and his misbehaviors, He chose to look beyond that, looking underneath, going straight to the heart of the matter.

Can't you just imagine that in Jesus' mind He's thinking, "I'll bet this lonely, rejected, outcast tax collector needs attention. He probably needs a friend. He needs acceptance." So Jesus said one of the most affirming, accepting things you could say to someone in that culture in that day, "Hurry on down from there, Zaccheus, because I'm going to your house today." He was going to enter Zaccheus' home and break bread with him. Breaking bread with someone in that day was more than, "Here's a slice for you, and one for me." They ate out of the same bowls. This is what was implied. "I'm going to go into your house, and we're going to break bread together out of the same bowls." This is what got Jesus into so much trouble . . . He would actually eat with publicans and sinners.

The beauty of the story is what actually happened to Zaccheus' behavior after that. It changed—radically! The Bible says that Zaccheus came away from the time with Jesus with a desire to return all he had stolen fourfold. He wanted to give half of everything he had to the poor. Did Zaccheus' behavior change because Jesus stood at the base of the tree and let him have it? Or did it change because Jesus looked beyond his faults and saw his needs?

As you're faced with daily parenting decisions, ask yourself . . . "What would Jesus do?"

*If any of you lacks wisdom, let him ask of God, who
gives to all men generously and without reproach,
and it will be given to him.*

James 1:5

Ask Yourself

1. Consider the statement, "Discipline means discipling." Think about Christ's twelve disciples. He took twelve men and "discipled" them. He imparted His life to them. How are you discipling your children? How are you teaching them to be responsible for themselves? Does discipline only mean punishment in your household? Or is there an element of training and relationship-building included in your discipline?

2. We believe that trying to enforce rules—no matter how "right" the rules are—without an established relationship prompts rebellion in a child. Parents, do you have an intimate relationship with your child? Do your children know that the parent who is implementing discipline is also the parent who loves them? who really knows them? Reflect on the amount of time spent with each child this week. How much of that time was spent in discipline? How much of that time was spent in relationship-building? A child can more readily accept discipline when he feels secure about the relationship with the adults around him.

3. Redirecting and disciplining wrong behavior is part of God's plan for our protection—whether adult or child. Do you see God balancing the meeting of our needs with the discipline for our behavior? What is God's "motive" or reason for disciplining us? How might this balance and motive be played out as parents?

Experiencing Truth

First Thessalonians 5:14 "And we urge you, brethren, admonish the unruly, encourage the fainthearted, help the weak, be patient with all men." This Scripture directs our response to certain behaviors. With a discerning heart this week, take a look at your child's behavior and the needs behind the behavior. We are to admonish the unruly behavior—or gently direct a child's disorderly behavior. We are to encourage the fainthearted—or to inspire confidence in our children when they feel "little spirited." We are to help the weak—give strength to our children when they feel broken or fragile. Through all our encounters we are to be patient—calmly persevering through the challenges of childhood behavior. Keep a journal for one week. Keep track of the different moods and emotions that your child displays. Also keep track of your responses. Are you matching the appropriate scriptural responses with their behavior? Are you admonishing unruly behaviors or neglecting them—hoping they'll go away? Are you admonishing when you should really be encouraging? How was your patience with normal childhood inquisitiveness, energy, and activity?

Special Thoughts for Single Parents

Discipline for a single parent can be overwhelming. Discipline taps into our fears and our aloneness. Having to face the challenge of avoiding harshness or permissiveness can be even more difficult when attempted alone. As a single parent, it may be particularly easy to fall into the trap of permissiveness. When we encounter the pain of a divorce, there may be the mistaken tendency not to set limits with a child.

You may find yourself not wanting to tell her no for fear of contributing more discomfort. But a loving parent is one that sets clear limits that give the child a sense of security. You will want to communicate to your child: *The marriage relationship may be different, but I am still the parent and committed to doing what is in your best interest.*

Special Thoughts for Blended Families

Accept the truth that you cannot control two households, but you can create a consistent environment for your child while he is in your home. Look for consistencies between the two homes and strive for more. Realize that part of your job as parents and stepparents will be to help your child deal with the differences. The rules of one home may not be present in another. One home may be more permissive and the other more demanding. Discuss these differences with your child and together think of ways to accommodate both. Also discuss your expectations for your children with your partner, as together you seek the "oneness" which fosters security. Are your expectations age-appropriate? Are the important issues kept important and the "not-so-important" expectations negotiable?

Finally, are you approachable on the subject of inconsistencies? Do your children have the freedom to tell you when they sense areas of unfairness? Are you willing to hear their frustrations over seemingly different expectations for biological children and stepchildren? Be proactive with this issue. Give your children the chance to share any of the ways they think they have been treated unfairly.

CHAPTER 9

Dynamic Parenting...Changing As Your Child Changes

A SIGN HANGING over a corporate executive's desk could just as easily be hanging in the living room of every family in America: "There's one thing that's permanent in this world—change!" How many times have you said about your children, or heard it said, "It seems like just when I have them figured out—they change!"

Time continues to march on, carrying you and your child with it. Changes come just as surely as the sun rises and sets. As soon as you think you "have it down," they enter a new "phase." Isn't it amazing how your child can go to bed at night as the child you know and love, and wake up the next morning and seem to be in someone else's body? If you have more than one child, you've also made the grim discovery that what "works" with one child may or may not work with another. Parenting is difficult! There's a great line in the movie *Terms of Endearment* that goes something like this, "Before you have kids, you imagine how hard you think it will be; and then you look back and wish it were that easy!"

Realizing it's impossible to fight all battles at once, parents are often overwhelmed—not knowing which ones to choose or where to start. Enter the world of "Dynamic Parenting." Tremendous confusion can be eliminated as "dynamic" parents come to view their child's journey through the grid of developmental priorities and learn to change as their child changes. These five developmental priorities portray a simple framework within which parents can focus their parenting activities and goal-setting for each child consistent with the child's age and corresponding developmental priority. This rescues them from being terrorized by every "urgent" demand and from expecting the impossible. Telling a two-year-old to "Love your neighbor" is expecting something beyond his realm of possibilities. "Put your truck back in your room" is an achievable request.

These five developmental priorities build on one another and must proceed in sequential order. They represent a healthy model of the process of "leaving and cleaving"—which, by the way, starts when labor starts! From that point on, the "dynamic" parent begins to release control in small increments. This affirms the child's sense of worth and competency as they learn to function interdependently with others and come to walk intimately with God.

Preschool Age: Compliant Behavior

One simple focus is addressed during this developmental phase, and that is compliant behavior. The goal? By the time a child is six years old, when she's asked to do something, she should do it. "Children, obey your parents" (Eph. 6:1). In an atmosphere of loving closeness, the child's "will" is shaped through consistent discipline from gentle and supportive parents.

Remember back in chapter 2 we discussed the developmental milestones of establishing trust (in infancy) and learning to balance the need for dependence and autonomy (in toddlerhood)? Well, these tools will now be used by preschoolers as they embark on discovering their world by exploring and testing new boundaries.

Having those steppingstones in place will make this first phase far easier for the preschooler. The child who has learned to trust authority figures will be ready to comply with requests, directions, and rules—sensing no threat or ill-intentions. Obviously, this is not to say that there will never be opposition. In fact, a significant challenge all parents face is how to respond in firm but gentle ways to the *inevitable* "wrath" from a child who is developing his own self-will. ("A gentle answer turns away wrath," Prov. 15:1.) But the road will certainly be smoother if the right paving material has been laid.

School Age: Attitude — Responsibility

Now our priority becomes compliant behavior without having to be told — and with a good attitude. We add to the foundation of compliant behavior the next two priorities: attitude and responsibility. For example, by the time a child is twelve years old, he or she can be expected to complete his or her daily hygiene "routine" without being told and without griping and complaining. When a parent has to constantly prod and goad their child into doing a routine chore, one might ask, "Who's the one trained?"

Attitude is related to intimacy and attachment, not necessarily agreement. Having a positive attitude involves a sense of community, a respecting of another's intimacy needs. Having a "bad attitude" carries with it the implication that intimacy needs such as respect, acceptance, and appreciation are being withheld as a retaliatory measure. A "good attitude," on the other hand, focuses on a willingness to meet these same intimacy needs.

If you want your child to do something with the proper attitude, he will have to be given a safe and protected environment where she is appreciated for who she is and affirmed for being the way God wants her to be. This hammers home again the importance of laying down that foundation of trust. She may not like everything you say or ask her to do, but she knows in her heart that you are on her side and will do what's in her best interest. This doesn't mean she won't ever disagree with you — but she will disagree with an attitude of respect.

How do you "teach" attitude? Actually, it's more caught than taught. What attitudes are your children catching from you? Do they see you modeling respect for your spouse and for others? Do they see an attitude of yieldedness to God when struggles and difficulties enter your life? Or do they see and hear grumbling and complaining—and perhaps even blaming? Do they hear words of respect and appreciation coming from your mouth or words of criticism and contempt? Is the appreciation conveyed for inner character strengths or simply achievements such as good grades or accomplished athletics? Remember, you reap what you sow!

At an early age model empathy. Teach your child through your relationships with others that other people have their own feelings and ideas. Respect your child's opinions, even if they don't agree with yours. Mete out consequences without blaming or making disparaging comments about their character. Provide a home environment that is more positive-centered than negatively focused. Have a "Can Do" attitude—one that looks at what we get to enjoy rather than what we can't do. Rather than saying no all the time, look for what you can say yes to. "I'd really like for you to be able to go to the mall. You can go as soon as you finish the dishes." Or, "I'd love for you to be able to go to the game. You can give Tim a call to pick you up as soon as your homework is finished."

Responsibility is fostered through parental example, positive reinforcement, and "backing off" to let a child experience the consequences of irresponsibility. A powerful example is sent by parents as they confess to their children when they've wronged them with unkept promises, hurtful words, or impatient anger. It also includes (and this is HARD—particularly for moms) giving them the freedom to fail. Rather than "nag" them about finishing their homework, allow them to experience the negative consequence of a bad grade. Rather than coming along behind them and picking up their dirty clothes off the floor, let them have the experience of finding their favorite shirt on the bottom of the mound of clothes that's been growing for a week in the middle of their floor. Most failures are not life-threatening, especially at this age. Praise your children for being willing to take risks, rather than always playing it safe. If they should fall short of their expectations, affirm their character strengths and applaud their courage to try.

If children fear condemnation or criticism, not only will they seldom venture outside their comfort zone but they will always be looking for someone else to blame for their disappointments. Again, Mom and Dad, they're watching you. What do they see? As they have observed the powerful and loving example of your "living letter" to them (2 Cor. 3:3), they will have been confronted by your testimony concerning the Heavenly Father. As they establish their own intimate relationship with Him, they'll be sufficiently prepared for what lies ahead. There's no greater act of responsibility than choosing to receive the provision of His Son; no greater empowerment of changed attitude than the work of His Spirit from within.

Warning: Change Ahead

We said earlier that one thing's for certain—CHANGE. A big one's heading down the track. At about age eleven or twelve, your child is about to burst onto the "Real World" scene and your ability to "control" him is going to begin to decrease significantly. It's easy to see, then, why establishing these first three phases in a timely manner is so important. Having *Compliant Behavior, Attitude, and Responsibility* securely under his belt will help him (and you) negotiate the adolescent years. [The diagram on page 148 will help you visualize the process that is taking place.]

Adolescent Age: Values—Goals

During the teenage years, a young person should begin internalizing a set of values, beliefs, and convictions that will guide his life journey. Believing something just because parents do won't prepare and equip him for life.

It's at this stage that parents usually begin claiming in earnest the promise found in Proverbs 22:6: "Train up a child in the way he should go, even when he is old he will not depart from it." Knowing that there will be many external (as well as internal) pulls, parents cling to this verse for reassurance. It's interesting to note, however, the verse

DYNAMIC PARENTING:
Understanding Your Child's Developmental Priorities

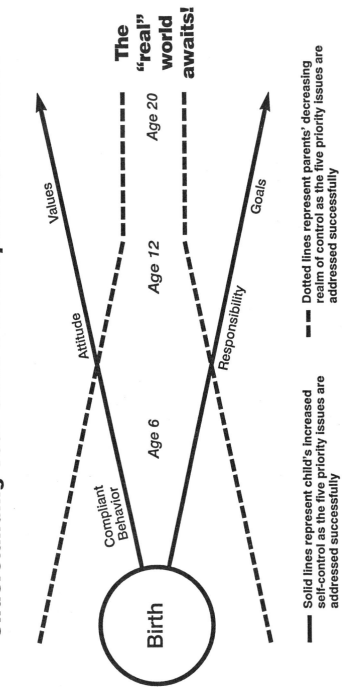

The "real" world awaits!

Birth

Compliant Behavior

Age 6

Attitude

Age 12

Values

Age 20

Responsibility

Goals

— Solid lines represent child's increased self-control as the five priority issues are addressed successfully

--- Dotted lines represent parents' decreasing realm of control as the five priority issues are addressed successfully

says "in the way *he* (could easily interchange *she*) should go." Notice, it does not say "in the way *his/her parents want him/her to go.*" Children must be allowed to pursue their God-given bent. Of particular importance here is the fact that teenagers must be allowed to begin to dream their own dreams, not those of their parents. They must be challenged to develop and fulfill progressively challenging goals and establish their own sense of life, vision, and purpose.

These objectives are encouraged by honest parental role modeling and vulnerable communication. Parents who have learned to listen give their adolescent a sense that it is OK to question and try things for himself without fear of rejection or ridicule. What better place to question, search for answers, and test ideas than under the safety net of home. Our goal as parents is protection—not control. We must teach our children how to think for themselves as they "leave" us and are guided by the promptings and principles of their Heavenly Father.

Every parent's nightmare is that their child will go off to college or out into "the real world" and throw away every value and principle held dear by the parent. When this does happen, it's often the result of a young adult being on his own for the first time who's broken loose from the tightly held reins of home. Never having developed an "internal" value system of his own or been taught to think for himself with God as his guide, he's pulled every which way by the enticements around him.

So, begin early to encourage your child to think, rather than just regurgitate through rote memorization. Provide an atmosphere that invites dialogue and the exchange of ideas. Parents begin to turn loose when they quit giving the answers. It can begin as easily and as early as responding to a child's question of, "Mommy, how do you spell _____?" with "How do *you* think it's spelled?" rather than just giving the child the correct spelling. Sounds like a small thing, but it's a beginning. It conveys a sense of confidence. "You can do this." As your child gets older, hearing things from Mom or Dad like, "What do you think?" . . .

"What would you do in that situation?" ... "What do you think God is trying to teach you through this experience?" conveys a sense of great worth as well as enabling them to develop their own system of values.

As the foundational layers of compliant behavior, attitude, responsibility, and values are laid, the structure is in place for the setting and realization of goals that are uniquely theirs. Caution: Parents, don't try to live out your unfulfilled dreams through your children. Let them dream their own dreams and reach for their own galaxy of stars.

Although only eleven at the time, Matthew spoke with the sage wisdom of one thrice his age when he imparted this insight to his mom. Consider . . .

The Case of the Dino Dig Discussion

Admittedly artistically impaired, Vicky has always delighted in Matthew's God-given creativity and artistic ability. Ever since he was tiny, she and Paul have provided him with opportunities to develop and use those gifts. When opportunity knocked, Vicky would point out to Matthew ways he might be able to use his artistic abilities professionally. Keep in mind, this is her dream, not his.

On a trip to the Jurassic Park Exhibit in Ft. Worth, Vicky was keenly interested in the fact that part of the professional team of each dinosaur dig is an artist who provides a rendering of the dig site. At lunch Vicky pointed this out to Matthew, who at that point was interested in becoming a paleontologist. Hint! Hint! Matthew could combine his interests in dinosaurs with his artistic giftedness. Matthew's response?

"Mom, I don't want to be a professional artist. It's kind of like with Dad playing the organ at church. He enjoys it. He's good at it. But he's not a professional organist. I like to draw. I'm good at it. But I don't want to be a professional artist."

Message received! Vicky needed to let Matthew dream his own dreams and set his own goals. By the way, Matthew has moved on. He now wants to be an FBI agent!

Eliminating Harmful Parenting Patterns

These five developmental priorities—*compliant behavior, attitude, responsibility, values,* and *goals*—are significantly and negatively impacted by two harmful parenting patterns.

"Neglectful" Parenting

Parents who are "underinvolved" with their children contribute to painful results. This "underinvolvement" can be subtle as careers are prioritized above people, making a living becomes more important than sharing your life, and even "ministry" to others is given priority above living your "message" at home. An additional issue is that your parenting role and responsibilities cannot be "delegated" to your spouse! (Pay particular attention, dads.) Moms can't "make up" for an underinvolved father. There's actually more said scripturally to fathers than there is to mothers. Be involved!

Compliant behavior through shaping a child's will requires a consistent investment of time to instruct, train, warn, and discipline. Healthy *attitudes* are developed through the powerful role modeling influence of involved, positive parents. *Responsibility* is instilled through daily tasks and resulting consequences. *Values* and *goals* are shaped as understanding, trust, and personal convictions arise out of intimate parent-child relationships. A child from an environment characterized by parental "underinvolvement" often grows up fearful of the real world since adequate training has not been provided. The child often begins to "perform" or "act out" in various ways in order to somehow gain the missed attention. Underlying resentment and an uncertain sense of identity are common in these children.

"Dominant Parenting"

Parents who are "overinvolved" likewise contribute to childhood pain. This overinvolvement might come from

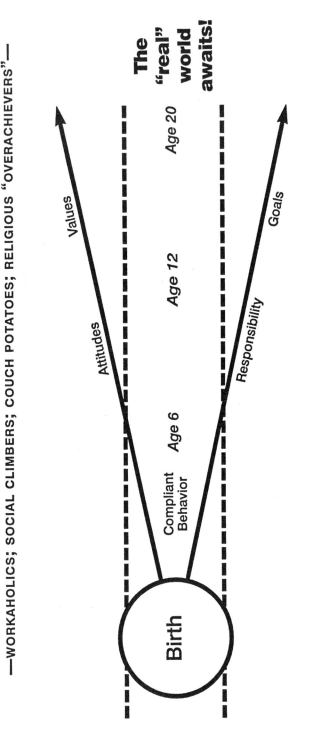

"NEGLECTFUL" PARENTING — PARENTS ARE "UNDER" INVOLVED
—WORKAHOLICS; SOCIAL CLIMBERS; RELIGIOUS "OVERACHIEVERS"—

The "real" world awaits!

Birth

Compliant Behavior

Age 6   Age 12   Age 20

Values

Attitudes

Responsibility

Goals

— Solid lines represent child's increased self-control and responsibility

■ ■ Dotted lines represent parents' realm of control and responsibility

excessive rules, anger/rage outbursts, and attempts to control the child—often prompted by the parents' own fears and insecurities. Similar results come from an "enmeshed" (too close) relationship where a child might be called upon to meet a parent's emotional needs or a parent seeks to relive her life through the child. The pain of enmeshment is particularly common as intimacy needs go unmet in the marriage relationship and one or both parents turn to children for affection, attention, comfort, or as an emotional confidant. In each of these ways, the child is hindered from developing properly in the five developmental priorities. Additionally, a high degree of fear and insecurity would be expected as the child senses an inadequacy in doing anything properly. Two extremes of behavior in the child would be common: (1) defiance and rebellion, or (2) fearful compliance with underlying resentment.

The Parental Fear Factor

Any change—even positive change—causes anxiety and fear (for child and parent alike). As children take on more responsibility and begin moving closer to adulthood, it can be a time of heightened fear in the life of a parent, as there is an increasing loss of control. Parents deal with the reality of their children entering a "scary" world where sin abounds. A parent has to deal with anxiety over possible failures and wrong choices. Discipline issues also tap into parental fears. Concern over "losing face," or looking stupid in the eyes of other parents or friends and relatives sometimes cloud a parent's ability to let go of the reins they've held tightly up to this point. "What will people say if my child fails or makes a mistake?" Kids can sense parental fears. The result? Insecurity. Self-doubt. In some cases, acting-out behaviors increase in order to appear "cool" on the outside while struggling with doubts on the inside.

It's important for parents to communicate with each other—to be journeymates. Talk with other parents. Don't wait until your children hit adolescence. Begin right now. Draw strength and wisdom from a network of support—

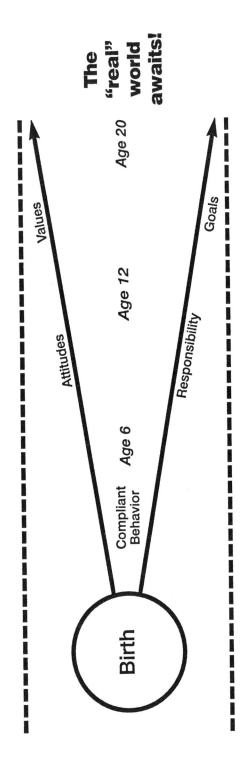

"DOMINANT" PARENTING — PARENTS ARE "OVER" INVOLVED
—EXCESSIVE RULES; ATTEMPTS TO CONTROL THE CHILD; "USING" THE CHILD EMOTIONALLY—

The "real" world awaits!

Birth

Compliant Behavior

Attitudes

Values

Responsibility

Goals

Age 6

Age 12

Age 20

—— Solid lines represent child's increased self-control and responsibility

— — Dotted lines represent parents' realm of control and responsibility

and especially from God. Remember, He loves your children more than you ever could and is with them even when you're not! Trust Him; let Him change and mature you just as your child is changing!

For God has not given us a spirit of timidity, but of power and love and discipline.

2 Timothy 1:7

Ask Yourself

1. How are you handling the inevitable changes in your child? How are you growing through their progressive development? Do you see any similarities in the "Neglectful" parenting model? Do you see yourself in the "Dominant" parenting model?

2. Take a look at the order of the five developmental priorities — compliant behavior, attitude, responsibility, values, and goals. Are you expending your parenting energies on the appropriate developmental task? In other words, are you trying to teach values when your child has not mastered the task of compliant behavior? Is your focus on responsibility that your child is not developmentally ready to handle? Are you taking initiative to plan ways to foster positive attitude, self-responsibility, and biblical values or are you just hoping they'll happen?

3. We know this may be tough, but consider your own progress through the same developmental model. What does your behavior look like? Can your boss rely on you to complete your assigned tasks without constant supervision? How is your attitude? How is your tone of voice? Do you accept the responsibilities that are yours? Do you take initiative when you see needs in the family, church, or work? Are the values that you preach to your children implemented in your own life? Are the values that you affirm on Sunday morning a part of your life on Thursday? And, finally, do you set goals? Do you set personal, spiritual, financial, relational, and family goals?

4. How can you make changes so that your parenting becomes more positive? How can you take the most current conflict over privilege or responsibility and deflate the power struggle by giving children a choice? Turn the "You can'ts" into "You cans." For example, your teenager asks to borrow the car and you know that her weekly task of cleaning the bathroom remains undone. How would you communicate your willingness to loan the car, but still encourage responsibility in her?

Experiencing Truth

Galatians 3:26 "For you are all sons of God through faith in Christ Jesus." Take this opportunity to remind your children that they have an identity greater than "your kids." They are loved intimately and abundantly by God, and they can be a part of His family. If your child is developmentally ready, talk to him about how to have a personal relationship with Christ. Ask for the assistance of a church staff member if you don't feel completely equipped. If your child already has a personal relationship with Christ, remind him of the Heavenly Father who is available to help.

Model your own accountability to God. As opportunities arise, share with your children ways that you are also responsible to God for your behavior, attitude, values, and goals. Confess to your child when you've "blown it" and then ask your child to pray with you. Ask for God's help in becoming the fathers, mothers, sons, and daughters He wants you to be.

Special Thoughts for Single Parents

As a single parent, you may find that the transition between these developmental priorities heightens the need for you to have your own journeymate. Change is a process, and change causes anxiety. Anxiety is much more overwhelming and incapacitating when dealt with alone. So give yourself permission to feel uncertain or insecure during these parenting challenges. Call a friend and share your concerns about raising your child. Talk with a set of parents in a nuclear family and get their perspective on the changes going on in your household. You will find that you also have much to contribute to their concerns about parenting. Remember, we're all in this together.

Special Thoughts for Blended Families

It may be extremely helpful for you to find a support group, counselor, or close friends to help you through these developmental changes. Trying to facilitate compliant behavior and positive attitudes is hard enough without the challenges of two different families. Plan to spend time discussing these challenges with your selected journeymates. You will find that you're not alone in these struggles and may begin to see the needs of your child more clearly.

A Child's Advice to His Parents

- I am a special gift from God. Treasure me as God intended, hold me accountable for my actions, give me guidelines to live by, and discipline me in a loving manner.

- I need your encouragement to grow, so go easy on the criticism. Try to correct my behavior without criticizing me as a person.

- Don't do jobs over that I have done. This makes me feel that my efforts don't quite measure up to your expectations. I know it's hard, but please don't compare me with my brother, sister, or other children.

- Please don't be afraid to leave for a weekend together. Kids need vacations from parents, just as parents need to get away occasionally. This is also a great way to show us kids that your marriage is very special.

- Give me the freedom to make decisions. Permit me to fail, so I can learn from my mistakes. Then I'll be prepared to make the kind of decisions life requires of me as an adult.

Proven Ways to Produce "Problem" Children

- Always solve his problems; go to the library and get books for him, go out and hunt down a job for him, tell him who his friends should be, and make his decisions.

- Be too busy with business, ministry, civic, or social life to spend time with your children. Or, if you do happen to have family time together, spend it, like seemingly everyone else, watching TV.

- Do not teach him the ways of God while he is young. Let him wait until he is old enough to learn to decide right and wrong for himself.

- When your child gets in trouble, always refer to a past teacher, church leader, or the influence of society as the real cause for the problems of your child.

- Leave responsibility for moral and spiritual training to the church and schools, but do not teach them at home.

- When faced with the choice of whether to spend your time and money on material pursuit, or on family "togetherness," always choose material.

Dynamic Parenting
Key Issues

Train up a child in the way he should go — Proverbs 22:6

Infancy 0–18 Months
Trust versus Mistrust

Developmental Issues

- Limited motor activity but very active senses . . . especially hearing, touch, sight
- Judgments made as to the world being "safe" or "unsafe" especially relationships
- Judgments made are primarily related to whether basic needs for food, comfort, nurture are met
- Judgments are at an emotional level prior to verbal/cognitive processing
- Judgments made of caregivers as loving, comforting, caring, nurturing or rejecting, punitive, uncaring, hurtful
- Judgments made result in close emotional "bonding" (trust) . . . or emotional distancing (mistrust)

Practical Suggestions

- Provide visual stimulation and soothing talk and music
- Nurture-nurture-nurture with touch, talk, and holding
- Lovingly and consistently meet basic needs with gentleness rather than anger
- Express joy; smile; laugh around your infant; pray "over" child
- Avoid raised voices, anger, over-protectiveness
- Remove a child from "problem" areas rather than discipline
- Allow child to have a "favorite" toy, blanket, as a security item
- Begin to take short times away from the child — expect crying; return with reassurance and comfort

---

Early Childhood 18 Months–3 Years
Autonomy versus Shame/Doubt

Developmental Issues

- Rapid development of motor, verbal, and language skills
- Autonomy needed in feeding and controlling elimination
- Approval of parents/significant others very important
- Differentiating between acceptable/unacceptable behavior begins
- Exploring/experimenting are essential to test limits
- Freedom to receive positive reinforcement says "I'm OK."
- Freedom to make mistakes and yet receive acceptance says "I'm OK."
- "I'm not OK" comes from overprotective, critical, demanding, permissive, neglectful, environments

Practical Suggestions

- Stimulate motor development in walking, running, throwing, climbing, etc.
- Read-read to your child; Bible stories, nursery rhymes, songs
- Provide a safe environment in which to "explore"
- Minimize "don't," "quit," "stop," "no" messages (some are essential)
- Praise and encourage every "success"; pray "with" child
- Teach-train-warn-reassure
- Discipline "rebellion" and not childish acts; firmly, but gently . . . without anger
- "Distract" a child from "problem" areas rather than overdiscipline

Middle Childhood 3–5 Years
Initiative versus Guilt

Developmental Issues

- Sense of competence comes out of freedom to undertake personally meaningful activities
- Inquisitive, fantasize and develop a functioning conscience
- Desire to differentiate from others . . . my, mine
- Initiative which is squelched by control or lack of opportunity produces guilt
- Listening to questions and fantasy is important
- Encouraging the freedom of choices is significant

Practical Suggestions

- Encourage and praise "favorite" activities and interests the child enjoys; experience Bible songs, videos, games
- Talk about feelings as you see sadness, frustration, fear, rejection—i.e., develop a feeling "vocabulary"
- Encourage social interactions with other children . . . at home, church, preschool
- Give choices about clothes, play activities, snacks, etc.
- Apologize and request forgiveness for your temper, broken promises, etc.

Late Childhood 6–12 Years
Industry versus Inferiority

Developmental Issues

- "Industry" is to set and attain personal goals
- Social skills have heightened importance in rules, roles, sharing, and sexual differences
- Capacity to reason develops and desire to be "useful"
- Sexual awareness grows and instruction needed
- Acceptance from parents, peer group, and other significant adults is important (teachers, coach, etc.)
- Lack of acceptance/encouragement develops a sense of inadequacy/inferiority

Practical Suggestions

- Find families with children the age of yours . . . initiate positive family friendships (i.e., positive peers)
- Explore and encourage hobbies, abilities, and talents
- Identify and praise personal responsibility and unique character qualities
- Special "talks" and experiences to teach social skills, i.e., manners, table games, social settings, etc.
- Continue affection from both parents . . . verbal and touch
- Begin open dialogue between mother-daughter, father-son . . . on sex roles and differences
- Share feelings; heal hurts; teach biblical principles, such as sovereignty, decision-making, avoiding evil, etc.

Adolescence 13–18 Years
Identity versus Role Confusion

Developmental Issues

- "Explosion" everywhere . . . physical growth, increased mental capacities, feelings, and hormones!
- Body image, sexual identity, and social acceptance important
- Independence, questioning everything and testing limits are expected
- Peer/parent conflicts common
- Interpersonal relationship skills, psychosocial identity and life direction help give "identity"
- Continual emphasis on competence goals in real life issues is important

Practical Suggestions

- Look for hidden needs and fears "underneath" problematic behaviors; admit your failures and share your childhood struggles
- Let natural consequences be a key discipline tool . . . i.e., give freedom to fail
- Continue positive family friendships with positive peer influences
- Ask "open-ended" questions: "Share something interesting about your day," — not yes/no questions
- Have special mother-daughter, father-son times . . . trips, projects, goal-setting; Bible sharing focused on real life!
- Focus on "Big" issues, don't make a big deal out of everything

---

Young Adulthood 19–30 Years
Intimacy versus Isolation

Developmental Issues

- Social relationships like courtship, marriage, and parenting are paramount
- Experiencing intimacy within friendships, then with spouse is a major priority
- Career, social, civic direction needed
- Intimacy development directly tied to identity issue . . . low identity, little intimacy
- Without a healthy identity, will move "toward" people in dependencies, "away" from people in withdrawing or "against" people in hostility

Practical Suggestions

- Guidance becomes suggestions from a friend rather than "rules" from a parent
- Discuss your "failures" and regrets openly . . . seek forgiveness as necessary
- Seek their input and advice in areas of strength
- Continue life training in real world issues . . . $, relationships, goals, biblical wisdom
- Listen more . . . correct less
- Dream together about the future
- Accept friends; offer protection and a sounding board about relationships (Maslow, 1970)

CHAPTER 10

Letting Your Child Know You and Your Marriage

AS WE EMBARKED on our journey of parenting with intimacy, we encouraged you to see your child as a gift from God—one to be unwrapped, appreciated, and enjoyed. We're now about to head down a slightly different, albeit parallel, road. Have you ever considered that you are God's gift to your child? Chances are good that you've never heard such affirmation slip from your child's lips, but it's true nonetheless. Just as surely as God has entrusted your child to you as a gift to be nurtured and guided so too He has given you to your child as a gift. You were hand-chosen by God to love and guide this precious child of His through the twists and turns of life. Just as your child is a gift that must be unwrapped, your life is a gift that must be unwrapped and revealed before your child. Parents' willingness to vulnerably disclose their lives is perhaps the greatest gift that can be given.

You are disclosing a lot about yourself and your marriage whether you realize it or not. We'll call this *passive disclosure*. Second Corinthians 3:3 says you are a living epistle, being known and read by all men. Who do you think is reading you more than anyone else around you? Your kids! Your child can feel your emotions, your moods, your pain. You can walk into a room having successfully conned your coworkers, the checker at the grocery store, your friends at church, perhaps even your pastor into believing that you're doing "fine . . . great . . . never better," but your child knows the truth. You can stay busy, do your household chores, and go about "business as usual," but your child knows where your heart is. So, rather than playing games, why not commit yourself to being real before your kids. That's what true intimacy is all about . . . and it's what teaches your children how to be real in a world that screams at them to live life behind fences and to wall themselves off from all that truly satisfies—relationships.

Three Faces of Intimacy

There are three different Hebrew words which are often translated "intimacy" in the Old Testament. The first is *"yada."* The psalmist uses this word in the sense of "to know"—to know a person deeply. Job also used this word when he made reference to the fact that even his *intimate* friends had betrayed him—those who knew him deeply (Job 19:14). This is the word that would apply to knowing your child deeply in the sense of knowing their intimacy needs.

Proverbs 3:32 uses the word transliterated as *"sod"* which means to reveal, to disclose oneself. That passage of Scripture says that God is intimate with the upright. He reveals Himself. He discloses Himself to the upright. So, first He knows us *(yada),* and then He allows us to know Him *(sod).* This is part of what was going on in the Upper Room in John 15:15 when Jesus looked at His disciples one day and said, "No longer do I call you slaves; for the slave does not know what his master is doing; but I have called you friends, for all things that I have heard from My Father I have made known to you." He had disclosed it to them. It's the beauty of the Incarnation that He became flesh and dwelt among us, and we beheld Him . . . full of grace and truth. Part of parenting with intimacy is dwelling with your children vulnerably and transparently—allowing them to behold you, warts and all.

The third Hebrew word for intimacy is *"sakan."* The psalmist uses this word when he says God is intimately acquainted with all of his ways (Ps. 139:3). This word means to be caringly involved. This addresses the issue of why God wants to know you—it provides the motive for

His knowing. Have you ever wondered why God wants to know you? What's His motive? Is it in order to judge you? To criticize you? To condemn you? Far from it! He wants to be intimately acquainted with you, to know you deeply, in order that He can be caringly involved in your life. That is a motive we aspire to with our children—truly knowing them in order to become caringly involved in their lives.

Three beautiful words that talk about intimacy . . .

yada . . . to know a person

sod . . . to let them know you

sakan . . . in order that you might be caringly involved in their lives

These three words serve as a challenge to move us from being content with passive disclosure of our lives to our children to active, purposeful disclosure. Parents, your kids need you to be more than just leaders. They're traveling a long and arduous road to maturity. They need mentors and journeymates. They need more than just someone to point them in the right direction. They need someone to come alongside, share "war stories" about their own journey, and walk with them. We're reminded again of the Apostle Paul's words in 1 Thessalonians 2:8: "We were well pleased to impart to you not only the Gospel of God but also our own lives." Parental self-disclosure ministers to a child's sense of aloneness and fear as she hurdles each developmental milestone on her way to maturity. It encourages and empowers a child's progress, catapulting her through difficult times. As the child navigates the sometimes tumultuous and treacherous waters of separation and individuation, the parent's vulnerable self-disclosure serves as an anchor to keep her from capsizing.

When—And How Much—Should I Share?

Just as growing up follows a predictable developmental progression, so does parental self-disclosure. Successful completion of earlier "intimacy disclosures" is essential for later developmental success. After a few words of caution, we'll approach each milestone, reminding ourselves of the key developmental issues facing the child and then look at the important aspects of parental disclosure for each particular stage. Before we begin our "disclosure journey," let's consider a few words of caution and encouragement.

As you share yourself appropriately with your child, it is very likely that some of your own childhood pain may resurface. Scripture calls us to maturity. This does not mean denying your pain, but it does mean having an adult perspective on it and not calling upon your child to carry your pain. If you find yourself needing someone to process this pain with you, find a journeymate other than your child—your spouse, a friend, a counselor, pastor, or support group. It's important for you to have someone to share with, but your goal in disclosing yourself to your child is not to weigh him down but to equip him for growth and forward motion. Remember our admonition in chapter 5 to leave your childhood behind? This is a new day, a new opportunity to break unhealthy patterns. *Carpe diem*—seize the day!

Parents are often hesitant to disclose themselves for a number of reasons. Perhaps the strongest reason is that they're not sure what or how much to share because they felt all alone themselves at these developmental stages. Their own parents were stuck in the trap of building walls around their lives and erecting fences to separate themselves emotionally from their children. Commit yourself to removing walls and tearing down fences. Let's begin our "disclosure journey."

Infancy (0–18 months)

As soon as baby makes his or her grand entrance into the world of bright lights and beeping delivery room monitors, he or she begins testing the waters to see if the world is a safe place. Looking for an answer to the fundamental question, "Can relationships be trusted?" Baby sizes up the situation based on whether or not intimacy needs are met.

Parental self-disclosure at this crucial beginning stage should revolve around communicating the following:

Acceptance

"We accept you into our family. You belong."

Care

"We're going to pay attention to your needs because we love you. You're important to us."

Joy

"You bring joy to our lives. We're so glad God gave you to us!"

You may be asking yourself, "Well, how do I disclose myself to a baby who can't even talk yet?" Don't sell baby short. From his (fill in *her* if appropriate for you) first waking moment until his eyelids finally grudgingly close in response to the Sand Man's persistent beckoning, baby is making assessments about his world based primarily on his interactions with you. Your best line of communication is through *tactile/sensory stimulation*. Your God-given five senses will enable you to connect with your baby as he begins to discover who you are and how important he is to you.

Touch

You speak volumes to your baby about who you are and what he means to you by the quality of your touch. Is it tender and comforting or stiff and forced? Baby is also learning that Mommy and Daddy feel different. "Mommy's hands are soft. She's gentle when she pats my back and strokes my face. Daddy's hands are big. I feel safe when he holds me. When Mommy puts her cheek against mine, her face feels smooth. Daddy has whiskers; it tickles!"

Hearing

"Mommy and Daddy are different. Mommy's voice is high; Daddy's voice is deep. Mommy talks to me all day long—

about everything. Daddy talks to me too, but he also makes lots of funny noises."

Though his vocabulary is limited, baby senses the meaning of your words by the quality of the sound of your voice. Laughter communicates joy and acceptance. Are your words ones of delight and affirmation or disgust and exasperation? Do you speak with animated inflection or in dull, wearied monotones? Do your words convey gentleness or harshness and frustration. It's not too early to heed the advice found in Proverbs 15:1, "A gentle answer turns away wrath, But a harsh word stirs up anger."

Smell

Mom, let baby be with you in the kitchen (obviously in a secure place away from any potential harm). As you prepare meals, baby will enjoy discovering new smells and will begin to identify this as a place where Mommy takes care of our family's needs. Let baby enjoy the smell of clean laundry and the fragrance of fresh-cut flowers. Dad, prop baby up in an infant seat or walker to watch you work in the yard or in the garage. Baby will begin to equate certain smells with Daddy that are different from the places Mommy goes.

Again, baby will notice that Mommy and Daddy are different. "Mommy smells sweet—like baby powder lots of times! Daddy smells like Old Spice—and sometimes like sweat!"

Taste

At age-appropriate intervals, let Baby begin to experiment with new tastes. "Mommy feeds me when I'm hungry. Daddy does too sometimes. It tastes good! And it feels good that they love me so much because they take such good care of me."

Sight

Provide a variety of colors, shapes, and designs for baby to enjoy, sharing Mommy's and Daddy's worlds. Trips to the grocery store provide shelf after shelf of bright-colored boxes and friendly faces. Riding on Daddy's shoulders gives baby an opportunity to view the world from a new vantage point. "Wow, Daddy's really tall!" Stroller rides and outings in the park provide a plethora of new discoveries for baby's eyes to enjoy.

There's an expression, "Mother's eyes are baby's skies." Spending most of his waking moments with you, Mom, baby watches how you interact with people and how you respond to situations. Baby is learning from you whether the world is a safe place. When a strange dog barks at baby on an afternoon outing in the stroller, do you yell at the dog and panic? Or, do you get down on baby's level, smile at him, and reassure him that everything is fine?

Early Childhood (18–36 months)

As a child begins the task of learning to balance autonomy and dependency while also resolving the issue of splitting (i.e., the Mommy/Daddy that loves me is the same Mommy/Daddy who sometimes has to tell me no or discipline me when I do things I shouldn't), it's important for your words as well as actions to model unconditional love. Parental self-disclosure should center around communicating:

Approval

Celebrate every little milestone. This conveys your approval of the way God has made them rather than the quality of the job. It is absolutely essential as they begin the process of separation and individuation that they feel your support of who they are, not what they do.

Empathy

An integral part of helping your child develop empathy will be your sharing thoughts and feelings that are different from hers: "Haley feels sad when you don't share your toys with her." Remember, don't equate love with her agreeing with you or even obeying you. When you see her sad, disappointed, or hurt, resist giving advice, lectures, or pep talks—share empathetic comfort from your heart: "I'm sad that you're hurting because I love you."

Faith

It's important at this age for your child to see that you are looking to someone outside yourself—to God—to help you. As you pray with your child at bedtime, let him hear not only your asking God to watch over him and to accomplish things in his life, but also your thanking Him for who He is, what He has already provided, and your confidence that He will do what's in the best interest of you and your child.

Protection

Begin laying the groundwork for your child's understanding that the rules and consequences you have for her are for her benefit and protection—not to cheat her out of having fun. They are an expression of your love for her. At this age, "teachable moments" frequently present themselves when your child is reaping a painful consequence from disobedience of some kind. When your self-disclosure is clothed in a blanket of comfort, it will fall on a far more receptive heart. Take, for example, a toddler who has just burned her finger on a hot stove. Consider these two responses and what they disclose to the child.

"I told you not to touch the stove! That wouldn't have happened if you had obeyed me. Go to your room and stay there until it's time for dinner!"

Or, first bending down to get on her level, you kiss the hurt and then say, "I'm sorry you burned your finger. I know how much that hurts. Let's run some cold water on it to make it feel better. You know, Sweetie, when Daddy and I tell you not to do something, it's because we love you and want what's best for you."

Middle Childhood (3–5 years)

As a child begins to explore the world in earnest, making daily discoveries about who she is physically, cognitively, emotionally, and sexually, parental self-disclosure focuses on three key areas:

Affirmation

First is the affirmation of their growing up and the new horizons that are opening up to them. This is the fuel they need in their tank to propel them through the doors of discovery awaiting them. Share your excitement with them and give them a glimpse of what they can anticipate. "Now that you're four . . ."

Also, affirm their uniqueness. Share with them the specific character traits you admire about them and help them see their value and benefit to others.

Confession

As you model a willingness to admit mistakes and ask his forgiveness, a child's sense of worth is enhanced and a greater sense of empathy is fostered. One afternoon David disciplined Robin for how she had talked to her mother but painfully the discipline was in anger. Leaving Robin in her room crying, David went downstairs to drink a glass of iced tea and read the paper. As God began convicting him, he began to rationalize. "Well, it wouldn't have happened if she . . . I'm the dad; she's the kid . . ." His arguments falling short, he put down his tea and went upstairs to apologize. Getting down on her level so he wouldn't tower above her, he confessed to her that he was wrong to have disciplined her in anger and asked for her forgiveness.

As a child makes discoveries about herself and her world, she must have the security of knowing mistakes are allowed. A parent who is willing to model that by vulnerably confessing his own mistakes, provides fertile soil for his child's continued growth.

Remembrance

"I remember when I turned four. Your grandmother gave me a Lone Ranger birthday party . . ." "When I was five, my favorite TV show was . . ."

As parents share memories of their early years, a child's sense of identity is enhanced, especially with the same-sex parent. [As an aside, this is an essential precursor to establishing same-sex peer relationships.] It's critical at this age for a child to get an initial comprehension that their parents were once that age, and that someday they'll be adults too.

Late Childhood (6–12 years)

During these years your child is continuing to make discoveries about who she is as she establishes her identity as the child God has created her to be. Faced with such weighty issues as sibling rivalry, competition, "fairness versus justice," and her need to feel successful in the eyes of parents, peers, and other adults, it's clear that parental self-disclosure will play a pivotal role in helping stay the course as particular focus is given to:

Dreams/Aspirations

Share your own dreams and aspirations at this age. No doubt many will match your child's. Did you want to be a professional baseball player? A jet pilot? A fireman? A movie star? A fashion designer? A beautician? A doctor? Challenge your child to view the possibilities as limitless and assure him of your support and encouragement. Dream with him. Now is not the time for cold realities and practicality. Grip his hand in yours as he reaches for the stars.

Decision-Making

It's tragic that so many children enter their teenage years with no experience under their belt in making decisions.

Admittedly, there is a risk in allowing kids to make decisions for themselves. After all, they might make the wrong decision—and then what? What, indeed! "What" is using those times as "teachable moments" to help them learn to link consequences with choices—positive and negative. Parents have an opportunity to share their own experiences. "I remember when I chose to _____ and experienced _____." Or, "I remember when I made a wise choice to _____ and _____." Sharing decision-making skills with your child and allowing her to make some decisions for herself facilitates her growing sense of identity and responsibility.

Share Struggles & Resulting Success/Failure

Provide an atmosphere that encourages your child to share his struggles and resultant feelings of success or failure. As you disclose to him your own similar struggles, connecting choices and consequences, it allows him to see that it's possible to make wrong choices and experience negative consequences and still "make it." In fact, one can actually grow from it.

A child this age perceives parents as having strong feelings of success. Disclosing times when you've struggled and "felt" like a failure reflects to the child that it's possible to have those feelings and still grow up and have a meaningful life. It doesn't have to be the end of the world! It's important for him to get this filed securely in his data bank before he reaches the storms of adolescence.

Hope

With the doom and gloom that bombard children on a daily basis in the media, it's important for them to experience hope from your experiences. Share times in your life when things have looked bleak and dismal but God met your need and caused things to work out for your good according to His purpose.

Consider . . .

The Case of the Now-You-See-It
Now-You-Don't Bike

In their family devotional times, the Ferguson clan had been talking about the sovereignty of God in the life of Joseph. No matter what happened to him, Joseph saw an event as coming from God and believed God would bring forth good from it. Joseph practiced hope!

For Christmas, Eric received his first "trick" bicycle—the kind that can do all kinds of wheelies and jump curbs. He was so excited! One afternoon after school, Eric went to the garage to take a spin on his new bike and . . . it was gone! Someone had stolen it. Eric had waited so long for that bike! To say he was sad would be a gross understatement. As he and David stood together, Eric looked out over the foothills and said, "Dad, I wonder how God's going to bring good out of this!"

Well, here's what God did . . . Eric's grandmother heard about it and gave him $50. The homeowner's insurance paid for the stolen bike. The bicycle shop heard about it, felt sorry for Eric, and sold him a new replacement bike at cost. So, Eric got a better bike and $75 to spare—and experienced God as One who gives exceedingly abundant above what we could ask or think!

Eric carried that experience of hope with him into his teenage years. He was about to go to senior high and didn't have a car. As August approached, he began to fret about his transportation options. Would Mom take me? Will I have to ride the bus? Then he called on his bicycle faith and decided not to panic. God would provide . . . and provide He did. Eric ended up with a multicolored truck the Friday before school started. Eric had learned to depend on God to meet his needs—sometimes God might involve parents in His plan, but it was really God meeting his needs.

Individuality

Share the things you did at this age that were uniquely you—hobbies, sports, etc. Affirm your child in areas where she is different from you as well as where she shares similar strengths and interests. It's important for her to realize that her identity is more than just being your child.

If parents don't encourage individuality at this age by sharing some of their own adventures in asserting their individuality, the child will tend to "perform" only to please parents and adults. This will ultimately not only stifle individuality but will foster a sense of resentment and bitterness. The drive to assert one's individuality is so strong that a child will find a way to do so, hopefully in a healthy manner. If thwarted, a destructive avenue may be taken.

Same-Sex Friendships

By sharing experiences of same-sex friendships—memories from the past, best friends and what you did together—you encourage the same in your child. Dads might tell about a fun trip or adventure that you and your best friend enjoyed together. Moms could share about slumber parties and shopping trips with a "best" girlfriend. This further facilitates identity, separation, and individuation, and healthy opposite-sex friendships later. Looking at school pictures and old yearbooks together can be a fun way to share these days of yesteryear.

Delayed Gratification

Is it any wonder that children who have known a life of one-minute oatmeal, five-minute rice, and instant pudding—not to mention having information at their fingertips within minutes on the Internet—have difficulty with delayed gratification? We as parents, of course, want to give our children "every advantage." And, yet, it is important for them to learn that all important things take time. Neglecting to do so sets them up for a rude awakening when they're out on their own and things don't come quite so easily.

Paul and Vicky were, well, let's just say "older," when

they married. Having waited until Paul finished his medical training, they had a few years under their belts. It was several more years before the Lord blessed them with Matthew, so by that time Paul was established in his career and they were comfortably settled in their first house. Their experience parallels many in today's society, as many are waiting until their late-twenties and early-thirties to marry and begin a family. In families like these, it's important for children to share, through trips down Memory Lane with Mom and Dad, some of the "lean" years.

They don't need to hear lectures about, "When I was a child . . ." They've heard it! They know how you walked barefoot to school in three feet of snow—uphill . . . BOTH WAYS! Instead, take advantage of some "family togetherness" times to journey back with your children to days both before and since their birth when things were different for your family. These can be great times of family fun. Consider . . .

The Case of the Ferguson Home Tour

David and Teresa piled Terri, Robin, and Eric in the car, and they set out on a tour of all the homes they had lived in while in Austin. At each house, they talked about what was going on with the family at that point in their lives. This provided an excellent opportunity for a discussion of successes and "failures" (actually, opportunities to experience growth!). Some houses represented bottom-line economic survival. Others represented sacrifices made in order for David to finish school. "Remember when we lived here? That's when Dad was finishing his degree in nuclear physics. Einstein was his hero then. Remember that huge poster he had of Einstein hanging in the stairway? . . . Remember these apartments? . . . These are the ones Mom managed. . . . This is the house where we had a swimming pool for the first time." At the end of their tour of homes, the Fergusons had spent time together— enjoying being together, reflecting on God's faithfulness, and being reminded that life is a series of trade-offs—ups

and downs—and often requires waiting . . . which is difficult for all of us!

Adolescence (13–18 years)

These years are ones of tremendous change. In early adolescence their thoughts, feelings, and bodies are changing
so fast they can hardly keep up with them, which at least
partially explains their incredible disorganization and frequent bouts of aphasia. In later adolescence, they begin
sorting through issues of sexuality and moving from depending on their peer group as a group to developing
deeper one-on-one relationships. Separation and individuation (i.e., "leaving father and mother," Gen. 2:24) are
major forces as they move toward adulthood. These kids
need parents and other adults who will be committed to
genuineness and integrity, qualities that will equip them to
face the future with confidence. Parental self-disclosure
should focus on:

Negative/Painful Feelings

It is imperative that your teenager begin to realize that his
behavior affects and influences others. One of the best
ways to accomplish this is for the parent-child relationship
to begin connecting on a deeper emotional level. As you
are willing to begin sharing your painful feelings, your
teenager begins to see the impact of his words and actions.

Eric had a habit of throwing his clothes on the floor,
even the clean ones. For years Teresa had been telling
him, "I get so upset when you throw your clothes on the
floor. You've got to be more responsible." Her focus had
been on his behavior. On one occasion she took a slightly
different angle, sharing her true feelings. "I don't know if
I've ever told you this, Eric, but when I go to your closet
and see clean clothes on the floor, I feel so unappreciated."
She was not judgmental but shared her own feelings of
pain. Her need to be appreciated had not been met. It was
the first time it had dawned on Eric that his behaviors had

the potential of positively or negatively impacting people he cared about. Up until then in his mind it had been an issue of, "Why is she in my room anyway?" Sharing at this new emotional level avoids a power struggle. It's disarming . . . penetrating to the heart of the issue. Do I care about this person I've hurt? Eric was being called upon to practice empathy, and his behavior began to change. He was being challenged to experience Philippians 2:3—learning to think more highly of another than he would of himself.

Parents often cover up their negative remembrances about their own teenage years by riding their kids instead. They're constantly on them because they're not bringing home all A's and B's. "You'll never make it to college. You'll never be able to get a decent job." Kids begin to tune that out. Instead, share honestly about your own feelings. "I wish I had worked harder because my grades really hurt me when I tried to get into the college I wanted to attend. Oh, I survived; but there were consequences for my negative choices. As a result . . ."

Ambivalence is looming large for these kids. In the same instant they both love their parents and are angry with them. They're excited about junior high school but scared to death. Everything that awaits them that's exciting also seems scary. Sharing your own feelings during those years will encourage them, and perhaps even provide some comic relief!

Temptations

Share with your teenager times when you were tempted . . . times you "passed" and times you didn't. Sharing such memories strengthens their individuality as well as provides comfort as you minister to their aloneness. It's best to offer these disclosures when they're not struggling with that particular temptation. Otherwise, it comes across sounding like a "lecture." "Family Nights" would provide an appropriate arena for such dialogue. Offer some biblical examples of people who confronted temptations and discuss what can be learned from their experiences.

Dating/Romance (Opposite-Sex Friendships)

Share memories of your first date, first girlfriend/boyfriend. This not only begins to reassure them that Mom and Dad are normal but also lets them see that the first person they date may or may not be the person they end up marrying. This can be liberating.

Parental Inadequacies/Admiration of Child's Gifts

Be willing to vulnerably share your own inadequacies and how you dealt with them. At the same time identify things that your child is better at than you are, in a spirit of affirmation. This will reinforce the legitimacy of her individuality and communicate that she is free to be her own person. It also models for her that she can be happy for a friend's achievements and abilities that exceed her own. This is hard for all of us to master. What better time to lay the groundwork.

This is an especially key task for fathers who tend to be more competitive with their children. The message is often given, albeit covertly, "Don't be better than me." Or, parents, try to live out their own dreams and aspirations through their kids and heap tremendous pressure on them to excel in areas that are of little or no interest to them.

God the Father blessed His Son with the words, "This is My Son in whom I am well pleased" and then the Son began to exercise all power and authority. Give your child your blessing and then free him to become the person God has created him to be.

Young Adult (19–30 years)

Your relationship with your children is entering a new phase. Now you are fellow adults. Although this is what you've been preparing them for, it's often difficult for parents to face once it arrives. It's only natural to grieve over things that will never be again, but embrace the new depth and breadth of communication that awaits you. As they leave home for school, careers, and marriage, your times of one-on-one dialogue will diminish, but afford yourself of the opportunities when they arise. Parental self-disclosure should revolve around the following:

Camaraderie

Acknowledge to your child that you recognize that you are now fellow adults, and that while you will always be available for imparting parental wisdom and counsel when he chooses to seek it, you also look forward to expanding your relationship into new dimensions of friendship and fun. (More on this in chapter 13!)

Negative Remembrances/Regrets/Confession

This is a tough one and calls for a willingness to swallow one's pride in order to do what is in the best interest of your child (your blossoming young adult). Share with her things you wish you had done differently and why. This is a courageous move because all parents, for the most part, do the best they can, but we realize along the way that even though our motives were good, our methods may have been hurtful. This demonstration of your commitment to truth will open doors of communication that might otherwise have remained shut and impeded your child's ability to develop vulnerable, intimate relationships with others.

The next step is to open up a whole new dimension of confession. After you have shared the areas you're aware of that are in need of confession and forgiveness, then acknowledge that you realize there are surely others you're not aware of. Give her permission to share those in love, genuinely asking her to reveal to you areas where you may have unknowingly hurt her. This is a vulnerable, selfless move, calling for a servant's heart willing to go beyond the natural desire to defend oneself to responding compassionately and repentantly in order to achieve a higher good.

David "dated" Terri and Robin from the time they were

twelve. On these father-daughter outings he helped them with their chair, opened doors for them, helped them on with their coats, brought them little gifts . . . role-modeling for them how they should expect the young men in their lives to treat them. When Terri was about nineteen and a student at the University of Texas, she and David were on a lunch date when he opened up this door of self-disclosure.

"Terri, I know there have been times when I've disappointed you or let you down. I wonder if there are any that we haven't talked about that might be on your heart. If there are, I'd really like to talk about them."

Of course, he was hoping she'd say, "No, Dad. Everything's fine." Instead, she said . . .

"Well, Dad, there is. Remember when I graduated from high school last year?"

David remembered. In fact, he scanned his memory bank, checking things off . . . "I showed up . . . I was on time . . . I brought a gift . . . We went out afterward as a family . . ." Things seemed to be in order.

"Dad, remember I was working part-time that semester. . . . The rest of the family went on down to the Berger Center where the graduation was to take place. . . . This may sound strange . . . but it felt funny that day to leave my job and drive myself to my own graduation. It would have meant so much to me if somebody could have come by and picked me up."

She was being vulnerable about something that had been inside her for a year. David's response was to empathize with her. "Sweetheart, it saddens me that that hurt you. I really regret that it did because I love you. I care about you; at all costs I don't want to hurt you."

"Thanks, Dad. That means a lot to me."

And it's healed.

Terri had just given David an important clue into how he can demonstrate his love for her. In years to come there would be many times when the family would be flying out for a trip together. David's faced with a choice. . . . Do we meet Terri at the airport or do we go by to pick her up?

. . . Pick her up!

Continue to search for ways to show love to your adult child by meeting their unique intimacy needs.

During one of our brainstorming sessions for writing this book, Robin revealed an area of hurt that dated back to her high school days as well. Although she enjoyed her thirteen years in a private Christian school, it had bothered her that she felt uninvolved in the decision-making process. It was obviously an area that needed comforting, because just sharing it brought tears to her eyes. David took the opportunity to go sit next to her, put his arm around her, and acknowledge the area of hurt and minister comfort to her.

As you are willing to make yourself vulnerable in this way, the doors of communication swing open. A sense of security is produced that invites future dialogue and promises a deepening relationship as you relate adult-to-adult. What greater joy could any parent desire!

Need of Grown Child

Parents never outgrow their need to be needed by their children. The challenge comes in communicating and fulfilling this need within the confines of healthy, appropriate boundaries. A great deal of the tension and conflict that arises between parents and their grown children grows out of this tremendous need to be needed. In fact, if adult children don't find a need for their parents to meet, parents will choose their own! Then we find the adult child moaning, "My parents are still trying to control me!" Or, "My parents are always critical of me. They think I'm still a little kid." In actuality, the parent is sending the message, "Don't you see that you need me . . . and I need you!"

At one point in his career, David's father was a building inspector. When David became involved in some real estate ventures, he was able to call upon one of his dad's areas of strength to tap into this need to be needed. "Dad, do you think you could inspect this property for me before I buy it? I could sure use your expertise." On an adult-to-adult level, David acknowledged his ongoing need for his father's wise counsel. His mother, on the other hand, was gifted in working with numbers. So guess who became David's tax specialist for the next ten years!

This is an area that has great potential for misunderstanding as boundaries may be perceived as being encroached upon. However, if healthy self-disclosure has been taking place at the previous developmental stages, the groundwork has been laid for open, honest communication. Parents, don't be afraid to express your needs, speaking the truth in love, while at the same time acknowledging and affirming your adult child's need to be independent. These can be years of tremendous satisfaction and fulfillment as you watch your child spread his or her wings and fly like an eagle!

> *Though youths grow weary and tired,*
> *and vigorous young men stumble badly,*
> *yet those who wait for the Lord*
> *will gain new strength;*
> *they will mount up with wings like eagles,*
> *they will run and not get tired,*
> *they will walk and not become weary.*
>
> *Isaiah 40:30-31*

Ask Yourself

1. What does your child know about you? Does she know what you were like when you were young? Has she heard stories about the way her parents met? Does she know the circumstances and story of her own birth?

2. Consider what you are communicating to your children, both passively and actively. What are you disclosing about priorities? about relationships? If we could look ahead twenty years, how would your children remember you?

Experiencing Truth

James 5:16: "Confess your sins to one another, and pray for one another, so that you may be healed." When was the last time your child heard you pray for him? Has he heard you approach the Father on his behalf? Does he hear your humility as you ask God for wisdom in parenting? Second, a child knows he is deeply loved when his parents respect him enough to apologize. Confessing our wrongs to our children lets them know that we have a Father to whom we are accountable. He lets us know when we've sinned and then we take responsibility for agreeing with God about the wrong. It is the same God who graciously enables us to do what we do right as parents. It is through confession and prayer that our families are healed.

Special Thoughts for Single Parents

Allow your kids to know about your own hurts. While considering their age and development, let them know that you hurt over the divorce. Express your regret over hurting them, but don't expect them to meet your emotional needs. Expressing your pain lets them hear the truth about the situation, since the uncertainty is often more frightening than reality. Reassure your kids that the divorce was not their fault. They did nothing wrong.

Special Thoughts for Blended Families

Tell your children about the challenges you face as parents of a blended family. Let them know that blending a family is difficult, but that you and your spouse are committed to doing the work. Verbalize your commitment to responsible parenting. It is not your children's job to work at blending a family. Relay this information with the motive of communicating truth to your children. Don't expect your children to meet your need for comfort or appreciation.

This may also be the time when you let your children know that you see divorce as wrong but forgivable. Acknowledge your own part in hurting your child through the divorce. Set aside some private time with each child. Give specific examples of the hurts your child might have experienced. Share your regret and sadness for her pain. With humility, ask for your child's forgiveness. Then share your hope because of God's gracious plan for healing.

CHAPTER 11

Preparing Your Child for Intimacy with God and Others

CHILDREN COME INTO the world issuing an all-points bulletin: "Hear ye! Hear ye! I'm here. I have needs—lots of them—and I expect you to meet them!" They burst onto the scene believing that the world revolves around them—and will continue believing that unless they are redirected. It's part of their fallenness. We all made our entrances in exactly the same fashion. One of your jobs as parents is to gently, lovingly wound their narcissism, redirecting and reshaping their focus.

The right side of the diagram on page 186 illustrates what this fallenness looks like. This "closed system" is ineffective because it takes God out of the picture, and it's impossible to have true emotional health without spiritual health. What you have here are two mutually needy human beings taking from one another. It won't work. Suppose your gas tank was running low, so you siphoned gas from your spouse's car. Later in the day, your spouse comes out and finds her gas tank is low, so she siphons some from your tank. At that rate, eventually both tanks will be empty—and so will our two mutually needy people. Healthy relationships need a never-ending source. The system on the left side of our diagram illustrates an "open system," drawing from an unlimited supply of love and comfort. The source? God who is love and who is the God of all comfort.

Parenting with intimacy is a call and commitment to move your child from right to left. In effect, you're called

HEALTHY RELATIONSHIPS

Emotional — Relational
Needs for Attention,
Affection, Appreciation,
Approval, etc.

God

Faith

Expectations

Expectations

Faith

Person

Person

Sharing Needs in Love

"Giving" to Meet Needs

UNHEALTHY RELATIONSHIPS

God is "sidelined"
as a spectator!

God

Person

Person

Expectations of Others

Demanding from Others

Hide Needs or Attack

"Taking" to Meet Needs

to help "drive out their fallenness." Sounds severe, doesn't it? On the contrary! It's the most loving thing you can do for them. Your goal is to drive it out—not with the rod but with your approachability.

Let's look at three specific dimensions of this process. [You may want to refer back to the diagram from time to time.]

Expectations and Faith in God versus Expecting and Demanding from People

Fundamental to healthy/unhealthy relationships is the issue over expectations. *Who* am I expecting to meet my need? Healthy relationships look to God as the One who promises abundance. Unhealthy ones, expecting another person to be the source of provision, eventually become demanding and manipulative. This is clearly seen in the Genesis 3 account of the Fall as Adam and Eve are tempted to look outside of God's provision.

As you seek to redirect your child's expectations toward God, you will find that times of confession and forgiveness are quite possibly the most life-impacting you will share together. You've let your child down. Perhaps it was a broken promise or a lost temper. You get down on his level, confess that you were wrong, and ask for his forgiveness. "I really regret that I've hurt you. I've let you down. It was wrong of me to _____. Will you forgive me?" Then take it a step further. "I want to remind you and reassure you that there is Someone who won't ever let you down. He won't ever disappoint you. And that's God." Now pray with your child, asking God to change you. "Help me with my temper; give me Your self-control." This can be a powerful avenue to take in reshaping your child's expectations toward God from a very early age.

Sharing Needs in Love versus Hiding Needs or Attacking

Since our fallenness has its roots in the Garden of Eden, it's natural to return there to discover the origin of our tendency to hide our needs or attack. When God went looking for Adam and Eve, they hid from Him because of their sin. When they were finally pinned down, they resorted to attacking and blaming. Children display this same type of behavior through such things as disruptive behavior and secretiveness, just to name a few.

One of the exciting things that we as parents have the opportunity to do is live out the reality of Ephesians 4:15 before our children. *"But speaking the truth in love, we are to grow up in all aspects into Him, who is the head, even Christ."* Sharing the truth in love is pivotal in developing healthy relationships as vulnerability and mutual trust are deepened. Provide a safe atmosphere in which they can share openly and model for them the appropriate sharing of your own needs. Let them experience your home as a secure place to share needs in a loving way. This is essential for the development of a sense of security. In this environment they have the freedom to be a kid . . . as well as the freedom to grow up.

Depending on the age of your child, you may need to help him develop a needs vocabulary. Many adults have difficulty placing names on their needs. Children shouldn't be expected to do this on their own. And remember . . . mind-reading is taboo! Train him in how to ask for his needs to be met appropriately. "I can't hear you when you whine. Can you tell me what it is you need? Let's talk about it. I really do care."

It was nearing four-year-old Susie's bedtime, and she was showing telltale signs of a hard day at play. First she picked a fight with her brother. Next, she began tormenting the cat. Hearing the escalating sounds of warfare coming from the den, Susie's wise mother made the most of a "teachable moment."

Kneeling down, she took Susie's face in her hands and said, "It looks and sounds to me like you might be needing a little lap time—and maybe a hug. Would you like Mommy to hold you?"

No sooner were the words out of her mouth than a big smile spread across Susie's face, and she leaped into her mom's arms. Susie was experiencing a home that was a secure environment where people loved her and cared about her and wanted to know her needs and respond to those needs. Even at the tender age of four, Susie was learning to say what she needed. This particular evening—she needed a hug!

And, guess what? We never outgrow our need for hugs . . .

Nineteen-year-old Eric had gotten up early in order to make his forty-five-minute commute to college in time for his 8 A.M. class. He gathered up an armful of books and headed for the garage. Just before he reached the door, he heard some clanging coming from the kitchen. David, awake uncharacteristically early, was making coffee. Eric and his dad hadn't seen much of each other over the past few days, and Eric had missed their times together. He went into the kitchen, put his books down on the counter, and said, "Dad, I need a hug."

Eric was free to share his need in love, having been the beneficiary of a legacy of love that communicated, "In this family, we want to know your needs; and we want to meet those needs because we love you!" That morning, father and son both received a blessing!

A child's concept of God is powerfully impacted by his parents—especially his father. How does a child learn to come boldly before the throne of God? It's modeled in a secure home environment where he is free to come boldly before his parents to confidently express specific needs in love, no matter how big or small. How will a child perceive God as approachable and forgiving unless his parents are approachable and forgiving? What a challenge! With an attitude of gratitude for the grace that has been shown to you, pass that grace along to your child.

. . . We love because He first loved us.

. . . A child loves because parents loved him first.

"Giving" to Meet Needs versus "Taking" to Meet Needs

Each of us comes into life with a huge fear that our needs will not be met. Therefore, we make demands—we "take" from others. Your role as a parent is to help cast out that fear as God uses you to take the initiative; "move first" and become caringly involved in meeting a child's needs. A sense of security is built as your child learns that her needs are met without throwing a fit. Take the initiative to model what God did on our behalf—He left His world to enter ours. We didn't seek Him—He sought us out. "Perfect love casts out fear" (1 John 4:18). Allow God to use you to bless your child. Learning to trust relationships they can see builds a solid foundation for trusting One they cannot see.

Mutual giving is key to healthy relationships...two people giving to meet important emotional needs; neither person "taking" from the other. Giving rather than selfishly taking is the crucial ingredient that brings joy and grateful appreciation. *"It is more blessed to give than to receive" (Acts 20:35).*

In contrast, nothing chokes out intimacy faster than feeling "taken" from. "Taking" is characterized by a very conditional love: *I'll love you if...I'll love you when...* This performance cycle is never-ending and never satisfies! Such relationships typically end up with two "bankrupt" people. Having to "take" never satisfies.

Cory had bugged his dad for weeks to take him to Toys "R" Us. His dad had reluctantly agreed, but Saturday after Saturday went by, each bringing a new excuse why they couldn't go. Cory was bitterly disappointed. Finally, Cory's mom took her husband aside one Saturday morning and said a bit melodramatically, "Either you take him this morning or he'll be scarred for life. And it will be your fault!"

"C'mon, Cory, let's go," muttered his dad unenthusiastically.

After spending about forty-five minutes going up and down aisle after aisle, Cory left the store with a sack clutched under his arm. His other arm was free, but his dad took no notice. On the way home, sensing that he had had to "take" this outing from his dad, Cory said, "Dad, thanks for going with me to Toys "R" Us. Maybe next time you'll want to go."

What contribution had this outing made to Cory's growing concept of God? An opportunity missed! Contrast this with the parent who proactively looks for ways to meet his child's intimacy needs and nurture his concept of God as one of a Heavenly Father who delights in meeting the needs of His children. Know your child and take the initiative to enter his world to meet those needs. To him, you're "God with skin on."

When You Sit, Stand, Walk ...

God intends for children to see the witness of these truths in the lives of their parents. Then, when they reach the age of accountability, the witness and testimony that they have seen and heard are used by the Spirit of God to draw them to Himself. In their minds, they're thinking, "So, this is the Person my parents have been preparing me to receive."

Here are some practical "how-to's" for living these principles day-by-day in front of your children, keeping in mind that redemption is always through relationships.

Deuteronomy 6:6-7 — Living

"And these words, which I am commanding you today, shall be on your heart; and you shall teach them diligently to your sons and shall talk of them when you sit in your house and when you walk by the way and when you lie down and when you rise up."

God gave Moses and the Children of Israel important insight into passing down the Word of God from one generation to the next. This passage describes an "as you go through life" approach to sharing the Word of God. This includes both a structured time of sharing and a sensitivity to "teachable moments," times when life's events present a prime opportunity for instruction. For instance, a teachable moment may be when your child is rejected by a friend and it seems fitting to speak of a sympathetic Jesus who also was despised and rejected. He taught us to love our enemies. A teachable moment may occur when the family pet dies and we can share about a Christ who wept over Jerusalem and at the tomb of Lazarus ... and who loved children and gathered them into His arms and blessed them. Encourage them to imagine Jesus' arms wrapped tightly around them, comforting them in their loss. When the family faces financial stress, remembering that Jesus promised to care for even the birds of the air and to clothe the flowers of the field in splendid array will be a source of comfort.

God's Word is what restores us from the inside out. As your children see God's principles "lived out" through Bible testimonies as well as the nitty-gritty of real life, your goal of pointing them toward God will be accomplished.

Pray with Your Children

Take advantage of opportunities to pray with your children. Mealtimes and bedtime offer predictable opportunities to pray together—to thank God for His faithfulness throughout the day, for special needs the child may be facing, and for things the family is asking God to do. Be sure to keep these times from becoming just "formalities." Seize other special times of great joy and struggle to involve your children in directing their thoughts and requests toward God. Don't try to impress them with the loftiness of your prayer. This might inhibit your child's willingness to pray aloud. Let them experience and become comfortable with the fact that prayer is just talking to God. Take opportunities throughout the day as things arise to suggest to your child, "Let's just stop right now and pray about that." This models for them the reality of praying about *everything*—nothing is too big or too small for God.

Vulnerable Praying with Your Child

This is truly a powerful force in preparing your child for intimacy with God. As they hear you praying to God, asking Him to change things in your life, seeking growth, seeking to be a better parent, asking His forgiveness for areas of sin (especially as they affect your child), this models the brokenness of personal responsibility and translates in your child's mind that she can trust you to God.

Confession and Forgiveness

As we've shared throughout this book, confession and forgiveness are an awesome influence in your child's life. Do not underestimate the power of a child experiencing a parent coming to grips with his own fallenness and asking not only for God's forgiveness but for the child's as well. The child experiences the freedom to admit his own mistakes — no longer bound by the lie of denial.

Journal of Gratefulness

Multiplied blessings are ours as we pause to "forget none of His benefits" toward us (Ps. 103:2). Regularly involve family members in a "blessing search" as each member names a recent blessing and assumes responsibility for sharing appreciation. Appreciation helps seal in one's heart the reality of the blessing as well as blessing and encouraging others. A few of the many benefits of a grateful heart are:

- Guards us from a critical, negative attitude
- Guards us from a judgmental spirit
- When expressed to others, it can motivate them to continue in "good deeds"
- When acknowledged to God, it is an important element of worship

A number of years ago, the Fergusons experienced this firsthand. When church finances and God's confirmation to the Ferguson family led David to continue serving in his position on the church staff without salary, keeping a Journal of Gratefulness kept the family's focus directed toward God.

Trust God with Other People

We often think that the ultimate goal of spiritual maturity is trusting self to God. "God, change me. Change my habits. I trust that You will do it." It requires much more faith to trust that same God with other people because you have then lost total control. It calls for a much deeper level of faith. Model for your child that God has put certain people in her life for a reason. God gives gifts to all men, and we can learn from them. Nothing enters our lives that God does not allow. This, again, will direct their expectations to God. Developing this faith perspective is an important part of what prepares your child for leaving father and mother to go out into the world. "Not only can I trust God with myself but others as well—friends, teachers, boss, spouse." Home is where they learn this significant truth as they learn to trust parents, trust parents to God, and see parents trust God with others in their life.

What Have You Done with God's Investment?

Our children are on loan from God. What have you done with His investment? Is your goal to keep them dependent on you, living off your faith? Or, are you seeking to point them to Him, preparing them for the day they'll leave your nest and try their own wings? When they do, they'll want to do so hand-in-hand with the One who loves them more than you ever could!

Let us therefore draw near with confidence to the throne of grace,
that we may receive mercy and may find grace
to help in time of need.

Hebrews 4:16

Ask Yourself

1. Consider the diagram that illustrates Healthy versus Unhealthy Relationships. In this chapter we attempted to communicate that the fallenness of man is responsible for unhealthy relationships. If you see your children as part of God's human race in need of redemption, how might that change your perspective? How might that change your attitude toward misbehavior? How might this perspective change your motives and methods of redirecting misbehavior?

2. Redemption is always possible through relationships. This may be a new perspective in regard to parenting. With this new perspective in mind, what areas need redemption in your child's life? In what ways are they demanding? How do they hide or attack? In what practical ways can you help deliver your child from his fallenness?

3. Parents could be described as "God with skin on." How might a relationship that focuses only on correcting behavior as opposed to building a relationship impact a child's faith? Since a child's concept of God is powerfully shaped by parental models, think about what you're modeling. Are you approachable? How will your children learn to come before an approachable God? Are you forgiving? How will your children learn that with confession comes His faithful forgiveness? Are you giving? How will your children understand His everlasting love?

Experiencing Truth

First Thessalonians 3:6 tells us that Timothy brought the "good news of [his] faith" to the church of Thessalonica. Spend some time reflecting about the good news of your own faith. How have you changed because of your relationship with Christ? What "good" things are the result of your relationship with God? If there are no changes, or you aren't sure that you have a relationship with Christ, then find someone who can help. Talk with a trusted friend, minister, or family member about these important issues.

Share your testimony with your children. Let them know the circumstances that led to your salvation. Tell your kids about a time when God answered a prayer. Share a time when God protected you or a member of your family. Let them know about a time when you experienced God's forgiveness.

Special Thoughts for Single Parents

If you are a single father, please consider the lifelong impact you will have on the lives of your children. What the male parent models in the home correlates significantly with a child's perception of God. If a child perceives Dad as absent, distant, or uninvolved, then his perception of a Heavenly Father will be much the same.

If you are a single mother, your influence over a child's faith is also important. But because of the strong, God-identification with males you may want to provide your child with positive male role models. You might want to establish relationships with nuclear parents, or encourage relationships between your child and youth leader or Sunday School teacher.

Special Thoughts for Blended Families

Your child may have some confusion about who God is, since he has more than one male or female role model. Acceptance will be an important area to model for your children. This may be most dramatically displayed as you communicate your acceptance of your former spouse. Do you demonstrate respect and acceptance or do you belittle, run down, or constantly make comparisons? How you handle this issue will speak loudly to your children.

Each stepparent will want to communicate clear intentions about his/her role in the child's life. You may want to communicate both by your words and your actions something similar to: *I am not here to replace your mother/father. I am here for you. I am here to give to you. I count it a blessing to be a part of your life.* Your child may begin to sense that he has two men or women who care about him and have his best interest in mind. He may even grow to see that he has a God who can take pain and turn it into great blessing. Your child could grow up feeling blessed in both homes.

Sermons We See

A Special Encouragement to Parents

I'd rather see a sermon than hear one any day;
I'd rather one should walk with me than merely tell the
way.
The eye's a better pupil and more willing than the ear,
Fine counsel is confusing, but example's always clear;
And the best of all the preachers are the men who live their
creeds,
For to see God put in action is what everybody needs.

I soon can learn to do it if you'll let me see it done;
I can watch your hands in action, but your tongue too fast
may run.
And the lecture you deliver may be very wise and true,
But I'd rather get my lessons by observing what you do.
For I might misunderstand you and the high advice you
give,
But there's no misunderstanding how you act and how you
live.

When I see a deed of kindness, I am eager to be kind.
When a weaker brother stumbles and a strong man stays
behind
Just to see if he can help him, then the wish grows strong in
me,
To become as big and thoughtful as I know that friend to
be.
And all the travelers can witness that the best of guides
today
Is not the one who tells them, but the one who shows the
way.

One good man teaches many, men believe what they be-
hold;
One deed of kindness noticed is worth forty that are told.
He who stands with men of honor learns to hold his honor
dear,
For right living speaks a language which to everyone is
clear.
Though an able speaker charms me with his eloquence, I
say,
I'd rather see a sermon than to hear one, any day.

Author Unknown

CHAPTER **12**

Preparing Your Child to Leave Home

AS YOU CRADLED your soft, rosy-cheeked, totally dependent newborn in your arms, do you remember what you were thinking? What your first words were? No doubt they were thoughts and words of amazement and incredulity, adoration and appreciation. Certainly not, "Precious gift of God, I want you to know that your dependency is only temporary. My God-given responsibility from this day forward is to prepare you to leave home." Sounds ridiculous, doesn't it! At that moment you can't imagine ever turning loose, even to the nurse who comes to return your little bundle to the nursery. And yet, that's exactly your mission: To daily build into your child's life, to equip her to one day chart her own course as she moves out into the world, independent of Mom and Dad. The goal was never intended to be for a child to stay under that umbrella but to eventually venture out on her own. We want our kids to leave from the front door of the house; we don't want them to have to escape through the back door or bedroom window. We want to equip them to leave confidently, optimistic and hopeful about what awaits them and assured that the WELCOME mat will always be out.

As you carried your newborn into the house for the first time, imagine seeing a sign pinned to the door that reads "Life Laboratory." God provides each child with a family — a laboratory of sorts where the child can experiment with learning about who he is, how he relates to others, and how to handle life situations while he is still under the safe umbrella of his parents' protection. As in any well-equipped laboratory, there are certain tools you will need to make available to your child in order for him to conduct these necessary experiments.

Selflessly Take Care of Yourself

This first tool may surprise you, but hopefully not. Hopefully, now that we've traveled as far as we have together on our journey of parenting with intimacy you might be able to predict that the first tool your child needs is that you know yourself and, in fact, selflessly focus on yourself. Notice that's self*lessly*, not self*ishly*. God has created this relationship called family, parent-to-child, in such a way that you cannot give to your children that which you do not possess yourself.

The last time you flew on an airplane, do you remember the flight attendant's instructions regarding use of the oxygen mask? "In the event the cabin should lose pressure, your oxygen mask will drop from the ceiling. If you have a child traveling with you, be sure to put on her mask before putting on your own." No! They advise you to first put on your own mask. Stabilize yourself first, and only after you've made sure the oxygen is flowing properly are you to put on your child's mask. Why? Because until you're under control you won't be able to attend to your child's needs. The same holds true in parenting. You must take care of yourself. You cannot give what you don't have.

As you focus on taking care of yourself as a parent, be sure to make it a priority to keep your marriage strong. As your child sees the strength of your marriage relationship, it gives them the freedom to grow up. A child's job is not to take care of Mom and Dad's marriage. The job of a child is to grow up. If Mom and Dad's marriage is strong—not perfect, but strong—that literally gives the child permission to do the job which God has given them to do. Why? Because security is present. When a child senses that Mom and Dad's marriage is strong, that if they have some difficulties they're committed to working them out, that gives the child the security, and therefore the freedom, to do the job that God has appointed him to do, which is to grow up.

The next element of selflessly taking care of yourself is to recognize the love, grace, and mercy that have been shown to you by a loving Heavenly Father. How many times do we look at our kids, expecting perfection from them, forgetting the love, grace, and mercy that have been shown to us? God has not called you to be a perfect parent with perfect kids. He has called you to be a faithful parent, equipping your children to become all they can be in Him. This is your mission as a parent, and there is no higher calling, no higher missionary work, than to be missionary parents to your children.

Affirm Your Child's Identity

No single factor is more closely associated with healthy personality development than what researchers often call "self-esteem." Self-esteem is sometimes thought of as a person's "mental image" of himself. Most professionals concur that as much as 85 percent of an individual's personality is formed by the time they reach adolescence. Thus, shaping a child's "mental image" is of major importance and, because of its early formation, parental influence is a major contributor. Hopefully this sobering reality will serve as a stimulus to encourage you to seek to understand the dimensions that form your child's "mental image"—or what we will call "affirmed identity"—and to learn the practical keys to building them into your child's life.

Self-esteem is one of the most hotly debated issues among Christians. On one end we have those who believe that self-esteem is doing whatever feels good, whatever you need to do to "actualize" yourself. That's not self-esteem. That's self-gratification, self-centeredness. And it never satisfies. Then there are those at the opposite end of the spectrum who believe that self-esteem is a satanic concept—that you should never think of yourself with positive feelings. In fact, we're all worms. Worms, worms, worms! That's not self-esteem, either. That's just another form of self-centeredness masquerading as spirituality. The focus is on "me." The bigger worm I am, the more spiritual I am. The true answer is related to our "identity" from God's point of view, with parents playing a crucial role to "affirm" this identity. It's understanding who God has created you to be, what the Scriptures say about who you are in God's eyes. Scripture teaches three essential truths that will lead to your child having an accurate view of how God sees her.

I am created in God's image

I am not simply descended or ascended from the monkeys or slime of the ocean. I am created, the Scriptures say, in God's image. I am a special creation. God didn't make any mistakes when He made me.

I am fallen but not worthless

Don't take a breath in the middle of that phrase, let alone separate the two parts of the phrase. Fallen, but not worthless. Scripture teaches clearly that we have all sinned and fallen short of the glory of God, but we are not worthless in His eyes. Our works are, but we are not.

I am supremely and sacrificially loved

There is a Heavenly Father who loved me enough to make provision for my fallenness through the sacrifice of His Son, Jesus Christ.

It is obvious that children are cherished in the eyes of God, so it behooves each of us as we seek to be faithful stewards of the precious lives God has entrusted to us to consider the three key dimensions that form this identity — and then seek ways to affirm this identity through meeting intimacy needs. These three dimensions — worth, belonging, and competence — can be seen in the Trinity: the Father declaring us "worth" the gift of His Son, the Son establishing our "belonging" as joint-heirs with Him, the

Spirit giving "competence" that we can do all things.

Communicate Worth

You've heard the good news about our worth: We're created in God's image. Fallen but not worthless. Supremely and sacrificially loved. Think about that! Our worth is not based in what other people say about us. The world would tell us our worth is based in what we have or how much of it we have. Our worth is not even based in what we do or how well we do it. It's based on *who* we are (created in God's image, fallen but not worthless) and *whose* we are (supremely and sacrificially loved).

"Worth" is primarily caught — not taught. Children "catch" how worthy they are as parents demonstrate through words as well as actions that they hold a place of priority that is not threatened by career, materialism, or personal indulgences. The paramount cost to parents is TIME! Time to be involved in children's activities and hobbies, time for family fun, time to listen and get to know your child, time to notice and praise your child's character strengths, time to offer explanations for decisions which affect your child. Without this sense of worth, a child embarks on a journey of "performing" and trying harder in order to gain this elusive sense of worth. Your child is WORTH the investment!

Build Belonging

The need to "belong" is so strong that it *will* be met . . . by parents or peers, by good influences or bad ones. Building a strong sense of family belonging is the best investment parents can make in protecting children/teenagers from unhealthy peer pressure influences. Share common interests and special memories. Laugh together. Vacation together. Work together. Belonging is built through the closeness of hugs, verbalized love, and words of endearment, and the establishment of family traditions at holidays, birthdays, and other special occasions. Sharing common interests as a family, special memories, and fun times also help build a sense of belonging.

A fun tradition the Fergusons have celebrated for years is a Valentine's breakfast. Their house is decorated with red balloons and hearts, and Teresa fixes heart-shaped pancakes with strawberry syrup. It has become such a highlight that Terri, who now lives in another city, still tries to make it home for the occasion.

Instill Competence

Gaining age-appropriate life skills should be taking place under a parent's caring and patient guidance from Day One. With each succeeding year, children need to grow in their sense of competence as new challenges are presented and "conquered." These range all the way from graduating from a bottle to a cup to learning how to drive a car and getting one's first job.

Although your child's worth is not based in what they do or how well they do it, their identity is, nonetheless, affected by the number of areas in which they feel a sense of confidence. A young man or woman going off to college or out into the workplace who can't balance a checkbook, doesn't know a saucepan from a frying pan, or has never operated a washing machine is going to feel somewhat apprehensive about his or her chances of "making it on the outside."

Remember these familiar lyrics . . .

Love and marriage . . . Love and marriage . . . Go together like a horse and carriage.   Let me tell you, brother . . . You can't have one without the other.

Well, brothers and sisters . . .

Worth/Belonging/Competence . . . Affirmed Identity
You can't have one without the others.

It's not catchy . . . but it's life-changing!

Goal-Setting

Involving your children in family goal-setting not only helps "shape" them now but also prepares them for the future as you help instill VISION. Enlist your child's input

DIMENSIONS OF AFFIRMED IDENTITY WITH KEY "NEEDS"

I'm **worth**...

Attention (care) as you enter "my world"

Understanding...get to know me, my character qualities, and my dreams

Confessing to me when you've been wrong

Praying with and for me

Respect (honor) my "space," ideas, opinions, and feelings

I **belong** to a family who gives...

Affection...verbally and physically

Acceptance...even when I fail

Comfort and **compassion** when I'm hurt, disappointed, or rejected

Forgiveness without conditions or rejection

Support through direction, limits, and discipline

Worth   *Belonging*

Affirmed Identity

Competence

I feel **competent** when you...

Teach me as we "journey" together through life's issues

Encourage me as we set goals and work together toward them

Admonish me with constructive guidance in what to avoid

Edify me as you appreciate my unique strengths and gifts

(depending on his age) on vacation ideas, hobbies, room improvements, or wardrobe. It's important for him to see that things don't "just happen" but must be planned. Involving him in family goal-setting ministers to each of the three dimensions of identity we've just discussed. They come away feeling . . .

I'm WORTH Being Included!

Spending even a few minutes to solicit input from a child or teenager reminds them of their importance and worth. Children can be expected to respond to goal-setting with varying degrees of interest, but when goals touch on items of interest, you can be sure they'll respond positively! Try asking for their input on such things as:

● What are some things you'd like to see done in your room? or with your wardrobe?

● Are there some friends you'd like to plan to get to know better this year? How might we go about doing that?

● Are there hobbies you'd like to learn or spend time on?

● What improvements would you like to see made this year on your bicycle, sound system, car, etc.?

I BELONG to a Family with Vision!

Including children in family direction will help them continue to feel a part of family life, even as they enter the stress-filled teenage years. Expect some initial reluctance from teenagers, but most will "come around" as they enter into family plans.

● What fun activity would you like to see us do together as a family?

● Do you have ideas on our family vacation this summer?

● We're thinking of starting a family tradition of having Valentine's breakfast together . . . do you have some ideas on what you would enjoy?

● What would you enjoy doing during some of our family nights together?

I Feel COMPETENT in My Abilities!

The more things a young person feels confident to take care of, the more secure they are in going out into the "real world." The fewer things . . . the less secure. Help them acquire new skills as they move toward maturity.

- Let's work on tying shoes and buttoning shirts.
- Can we work together on cooking breakfast this month?
- Let's work on answering the telephone and mailing letters this summer.
- Next week during family night we're going to change a flat tire and check the oil in the car.
- Let's open up a bank account for you, and learn how to balance a checkbook.
- Why don't you help me sort the clothes, and we'll do the laundry together.

Money Management

How many times have you heard of a young man or woman going off to college, receiving a "preapproved" credit card from an altruistic credit card company, and then getting themselves hopelessly in debt? And how many parents receive late-night calls with pleas for "Send more money!" Sad to say, these are not rare occurrences. It's important to start early in teaching your child how to manage money.

An allowance is an effective learning tool. Moms and Dads should agree together on the amount, which should be appropriate for the child's age. Giving an allowance is most effective when it is not tied to specific chores or responsibilities. These are issues of personal responsibility as the child functions as a contributing member of the family. An allowance is to give her an opportunity to learn how to manage money, and shouldn't be associated with rewards and punishments. Assuming her intentions are not illegal or immoral, how she spends it should be left up to her. And when it's gone—it's gone. And before she leaves home, she should have an established savings and checking account.

Dads and Moms . . . Eyes are watching! What are they seeing in terms of the way you handle and manage money? Sobering thought!

Friendships

While it's true that you can't pick your child's friends, you can be influential in a number of ways. First, be proactive in developing friendships with families who share similar moral and spiritual values. What better way for your child to learn how to make and develop friendships than to watch his parents in action. Qualities of loyalty, generosity, and other-centeredness can be modeled.

One of Teresa and David's special blessings has been their friendship with the Oliver family. Born only ten days apart, Eric and David Oliver became good friends as the two families spent time together. David and Eric attended the same elementary school, terrorized the same middle school principal, and currently spend time together on double dates. As they grew into dolescence and young adulthood, it was their mutual encouragement of one another that often kept them on the "right track." At times more important than parents' counsel and exhortation was their caring commitment to each other.

Guide Them Down the Narrow Path

You're preparing your child to enter a success-crazed world. Visit any bookstore and you'll discover shelves full of books on how to be successful. We're constantly barraged with an emphasis on getting more done, dressing for success, and winning friends. Yet it's possible, in spite of all this good advice, that we may be missing some of the real secrets of how to be successful. *Good* things are often the worst enemies of the *best* things.

A story about George Mueller, a nineteenth-century minister, orphanage director, and author tells about a time when he was asked about his secrets for success. He answered, "As I look back on my life, what I see is that I was constantly brought to crossroads in my life—crossroads which demanded a choice of which way I should go. As I was brought to those crossroads, I believe the key to my success is that I seemed to have consistently chosen the *least traveled path*."

There's a broad road out there. It's a wide pathway where many, and maybe most, travel. Let's take a look at three secrets of the narrow pathway that we can impart to our children as they prepare to choose which path they will travel.

PEOPLE Are More Important Than PROJECTS

Keeping this priority is a constant challenge. Too often we view people as no more than cogs in our wheel of success. We place people in a ranking of nothing more than projects, tasks, and things to be dealt with, forgetting that they too have emotions, feelings, goals, problems, and families of their own. These people can be classmates, employees, bosses, fellow workers or, worse still, family members or friends.

This principle explains why technicians sometimes don't make good sales people—they are too enamored with the "Whiz!/Bang!" of how *things* work . . . they tend to miss the "people" around them! A major challenge of the high-tech world in which we live is confronting the cold, calculating, and callous attitudes which result from working with equipment and paper rather than people.

How do your kids see you viewing the people in your life? As steppingstones on the way to success? As merely a means to an end? As competition and complications?

ATTITUDE Is More Important Than APTITUDE

There's great debate in society today over which is more important, attitude or aptitude. An important admonition to remember when this question arises is, "For as he thinks . . . so is he" (Prov. 23:7). Would you rather hire a good-natured, loyal, hard-working, and dedicated person who does his/her best or someone who is disloyal, lazy, and rebellious, but who has an exceedingly great aptitude?

A deep impression was made on David by a wise boss in one of his first jobs when one day he was asked, "Now that you've been here for a year, have you observed that there are two kinds of people out there?"

David began trying to categorize people in his mind: tall, short; bright, slow; Republicans, Democrats; men, women. Then Mr. Carlson, the wise boss, added, "There are those with a 'Can Do' attitude and those with an 'I Can't' attitude."

Attitude is crucial to success. What kind of attitude do your kids see in you? Commit to cultivating an "I Can" attitude and gather like-minded individuals around you.

It's interesting that in our day there's so much emphasis placed on self-improvement, training, and skill development, but so little attention paid to attitude development. It's interesting, when you think about it, because you'll find that you can change your attitude more quickly than you can change your aptitude (through education, experience, etc.). In fact, some of your aptitudes won't change no matter what you do. So we should all quit majoring on the "minors" and begin to major on attitude. Things can be different.

CHARACTER Is More Important Than CASH

Character is more important than things, bank accounts, or "stuff." Your *word* is more important than a shady, yet profitable, deal. Your *reputation* is more important than your compromised character. We frequently ask new acquaintances, "What do you do?" A far more important question is, "Who are you?" Our kids are reading where we place our emphasis. Focus on character. Be more interested in a person's dreams, desires, beliefs, convictions — who they are — than in what they do. A person's whole outlook can change drastically when this is done.

When Charles was in his early twenties, he set a goal to become a millionaire by the time he was thirty. So he worked on all his projects, his aptitudes, and his cash. And at the age of thirty he reached his goal. He was a millionaire. He went through life prioritizing projects, aptitude, and things, and in the meantime he lost his family, his friends, his health, and nearly his sanity. He had viewed people merely as steppingstones to his success.

In his later years of life, he began to deal with the question, "Who am I?" He began some self-examination. He knew *what* he was—a multimillionaire. But *who* exactly was he? It was at this point that he made some deeply significant redirections and discoveries in his life. At age seventy-two, Charles made a personal commitment of his life to Jesus Christ. He testified that at an early age he saw a ladder he wanted to climb, so he climbed it. But, when he got to the top, and he did get to the top, he looked around and discovered that his ladder was leaning against the wrong wall! He found life at the top of his ladder empty and lonely.

Perhaps these three secrets will help you climb the right ladder and place your priorities in the proper perspective. As you lean your ladder against the right wall, your child is more likely to want to lean hers next to yours.

Train up a child in the way he should go,
even when he is old he will not depart from it.

Proverbs 22:6

Ask Yourself

1. Consider your relationship with your young adult. Is the relationship beginning to look like a friendship? Can you identify your own strengths and weaknesses? Have you celebrated the strengths and weaknesses of your child? Are there conflicts that need to be resolved in order for a friendship to be developed? Are there too many ties to home? Does your young adult seem confident to handle himself/herself outside your home?

2. What interests could you and your teenager find in common? Find something that the two of you can do together.

You may have to look past gender stereotypes and develop an interest that is unique. Moms may enjoy learning to do car repairs along with their teenage sons. Fathers might enjoy polishing their skills in the kitchen beside their daughters. Whatever the areas of common interest, are they building a mutual respect and appreciation for one another? Are you also able to respect areas of interest that you don't have in common?

3. Have you initiated a conversation with your young adult that addresses her hurts from childhood? What might be preventing you from approaching your child? When can you schedule a time to do this?

Experiencing Truth

First Peter 2:17 "Honor all men." Make a special effort to communicate respect to your young adult. Respect his schedule. Ask about his plans for the week. When will he need the car? When do you need to change dinner plans? Work out scheduling difficulties within the family ahead of time. Next, respect your teen's privacy. Be sure to knock before you enter his room or bathroom. Ask permission before you read or look at personal items. Ask permission before you share personal information about your teen with your friends. Finally, respect your child's opinions. Listen to his ideas. Hear his objections with an open mind. Stand firm on your expectations of what you want done, but give choices about the "whens" and "hows."

Special Thoughts for Single Parents

When your child reaches the teenage years and is preparing for adulthood, you must begin to make some preparations yourself. It will be extremely important for you to begin to build a life apart from your child. Establish your own friends, companions, and interests. Developing your own world will give your child permission to grow up. You will help prevent the feelings of responsibility they might feel for you. Make plans now to build or strengthen peer relationships in order to defend against the times of aloneness in the future.

This is also the time you may want to encourage your child to further develop her relationship with your ex-spouse. If they've not had it before, your teenager needs the time with the other parent to discover this parent's strengths and weaknesses. She needs to dispel the notion that the other parent is "perfect." It will be difficult for your child to grow up and "leave father and mother" unless she's had a relationship with father and mother.

Special Thoughts for Blended Families

With all the work that has gone into blending a family, it may be difficult to shift gears. You must begin letting go. Along with your mate, start planning for the time when your teenager leaves home. Start refocusing on marriage issues and recultivating couple friends. Again, you'll want to give your child freedom to leave home without the feelings of responsibility for parents' emotions.

You will want to address any hurt or pain that your child may have suffered from the divorce. Initiate conversations that give your teenager the opportunity to grieve over the broken home. Ask him what he missed. Let him tell you what he regrets. This grief work may be uncomfortable, but it is a necessary task for growing up.

CHAPTER 13

Relating to Your Adult Children & the Blessing of Grandchildren

YOUR EAGLET HAS flown from the nest. As you've traveled this road of parenting with intimacy there have been times when you couldn't wait for this day to come—and thought it never would. Now that it's here, you undoubtedly greet it with mixed emotions. Elated that the foundation's been laid and they're finally "on their own," you also find yourself feeling a sense of loss and sadness. Both are to be expected—and celebrated! Celebrate the dawning of a new day of your parenting with intimacy journey. This may, however, be the most difficult leg yet of your journey. Letting go is always harder (and scarier) than holding on because it requires relinquishing control. It's kind of like when your teenager took driver's education and had his instructor sitting right next to him with access to an extra emergency brake—"just in case." But once he got that license and headed down the road solo, he was at the controls.

This leg of your journey requires a tremendous amount of trust—trust in yourself that you've done the best you could, trust in your now-grown child, trust in the foundation of intimacy and responsibility that has been laid and, most importantly, trust in the God who created her, uniquely gifted her for the road He intends her to travel and who loves her with a love beyond our human comprehension.

As we discussed in our last chapter, you've been preparing your child for the day he would leave your nest since you brought him home from the hospital. Dependency was never intended to be a permanent state. The welcome mat is always out, but it's time to shift into a different gear. The doors of the old homestead should be open as a welcome rest stop for times of refueling but not available as a rescue station to retreat from responsibility. Autonomy with attachment is the order of the day.

One of the greatest "parting gifts" you can give to your adult child is the strength of your own marriage. It frees her to leave home without feeling responsible for either keeping your marriage together or meeting your emotional needs. It's significant that your "newly adult" children see and hear of your fun couple times together, new common interests, and fresh dreams for the future. Don't underestimate the value of this gift . . . it's truly the gift that keeps on giving.

A Tried-and-True Family Recipe

Just because your "child" has left home doesn't mean he's lost his taste for home cooking. In fact, he probably craves it more than ever! Our "Recipe for Closeness" in chapter 4 with its four basic ingredients—Affectionate Caring, Vulnerable Communication, Joint Accomplishment, and Mutual Giving—will continue to be a family favorite when served in appropriate portions. Of course, as family dynamics change, you'll need to modify the seasonings to appeal to changing tastes and discriminating palates. A word of caution to the cook: Although tempting to do so, avoid overseasoning. In other words, examine your motives and respect boundaries.

Affectionate Caring

Your adult child's intimacy needs don't cease to exist when she walks out your front door. As she encounters the harsh realities of life, in fact, her need for such things as encouragement, approval, support, and comfort rise quickly to the surface. While there are now others in her life who have perhaps taken a more prominent role in meeting these needs, you can certainly continue to have a vital role through thoughtful notes of encouragement, special cards, and occasional phone calls. Conveying your support and confidence through messages that say, "I love you! . . . We're thinking about you! . . . You can do it! . . . We believe in you! . . . Go for it! . . . We'll be praying for you! . . ." provide an opportunity to give those hugs and pats on the back even when not physically able to do so.

Some families establish regular times for telephone "updates," maybe alternating who initiates the call—parents this week, son or daughter next week; others share written updates as reunion visits are planned and anticipated. Even though parents might be tempted to think verbalized love would be less important—just the opposite is likely true. Since our "newly adult" children are not as available to sense our love through daily care and support, verbalized love may be more significant—you'll need to express love to son-in-law/daughter-in-law and eventually grandchildren. Most "newly adult" children would express preference for the more vulnerable "I love you" than "we" love you.

Vulnerable Communication

As your adult child encounters certain life situations, things will come to the surface related to his past that will need to be addressed. Keep your defenses down, use these as opportunities for open, honest sharing. Your commitment to the truth and willingness to work through issues will further deepen the level of trust in your relationship. And as trust is deepened, you will be able to share in their fears, disappointments, and dreams. Emotional responding and confession and forgiveness will be welcome companions as you travel down these new roads of communication. Use them generously and wisely, and you'll reap the rewards.

After Terri left home, David found that he was extremely disappointed when everyone was not together for family get-togethers. Because of the pressure she felt, Terri began to feel disrespected and resentful of the guilt she felt because she had "disappointed" her dad. David came to realize that part of his driving need to have everyone together was the result of his awareness that he had "messed up" in some areas earlier in his family's life and he hadn't finished dealing with it. So, he was trying to "make up" for his mistakes by insisting that everyone be together. As he began to process what was really going on, he asked himself, "Can I trust God to take care of this?" Of course, the answer was yes, and as he did so he was released and able to give Terri as well as other family members the freedom they needed. Practicing vulnerable communication, David could then say, "I would sure love for you to be here, but I understand your desire to be with your friends. I'll miss you, but I hope you have a great time. I'll be anxious to hear about it."

Joint Accomplishment

Develop common interests such as sports, hobbies, shopping, or cooking. Look for things you can enjoy doing together in an atmosphere devoid of unhealthy competitiveness and the need to control. Vacation together when schedules allow and let them know they're welcome at family functions. As noted in the Ferguson's example above, they must be given the freedom to establish their own friendships, schedules, and traditions.

The Fergusons have a number of fun card and domino games that bring the family together for a little friendly competition. Family trips together provide other opportunities for working together as a team: Terri takes charge of planning all cultural activities; Robin is the designated photographer; Ike is the trip navigator while Eric is in charge of entertaining the family with trivia, one-liners, and practical jokes.

Other opportunities for the Fergusons to jointly work toward goals include Terri's role as home decorating consultant, Robin's role as family "historian," and Teresa's role as fashion coordinator. The male "team" enjoys golfing together, computer gadgetry, and sporting events.

Mutual Giving

Developmentally, your relationship can now move to a level where it is characterized by reciprocity — a give-and-take between adults. As their adult children leave home, parents may fear that their need to be needed will no longer be met — so they begin "taking." The result is resentment on all sides. Practice sharing your needs in love and head resentment off at the pass. Be willing to "receive" from your grown child. Parents who are unwilling to do so will find their sense of aloneness heightened. Practice mutual giving and enjoy the rewards.

Several years ago, Teresa and David had just finished conducting a four-day "Marriage Intensive." They were exhausted! Driving home on a Saturday afternoon, their car phone rang. It was Eric.

"Mom, what are you doing?"

"We're on our way home from an Intensive," Teresa responded.

"What do y'all have planned tonight?" Now this is a Saturday night. Eric is nineteen years old at this time and has been dating Meleah for a little over a year. "If it's OK with you and Dad, Meleah and I would like to come over tonight and play cards with you. When I talked to Meleah this morning, that's what she wanted to do."

Do you think that might bless your heart as a parent? A nearly grown son who wants to invite his girlfriend over on Saturday evening for games with his parents! Mutual giving. Eric felt the security of enjoying family time together plus the blessing of giving back to his parents — the gift of his time, of his love, of his girlfriend — from an attitude of gratitude for all that had been given to him.

David was blessed just recently by a phone call from Terri. He and Teresa had just arrived home from a major meeting with Dr. Bill and Vonette Bright of Campus Crusade for Christ concerning the Intimate Life ministry. Terri had just called to "check-in" on Mom and Dad, desiring to communicate her interest and support. David would comment: "It felt like the tables were turned; it wasn't

Teresa and me checking in with Terri on decisions or news about her life, instead she was blessing us with her caring interest and support." Surely this must be part of what the psalmist had in mind when he spoke of children being a gift from the Lord (Ps. 127:3).

When Wedding Bells Ring...

Call to mind every intimacy principle you've gleaned so far, and then apply them lovingly to your relationship with your new son- or daughter-in-law. Realize that not only have two unique personalities been united but two divergent backgrounds as well. Instead of resenting new traditions, celebrate and support them. When you're tempted to feel like this son- or daughter-in-law has seemingly "stolen" your "child" from long-standing family traditions and holidays, remember this is an important part of "leaving and cleaving." Be "grown up" enough to realize that they may not do things the way your family has always done them...and that's OK! Allow them to make the same wonderful discovery of unwrapping their gifts that you discovered throughout the years your child lived under your roof.

As misunderstandings arise or words are misconstrued, practice those principles of emotional responding, vulnerable communication, confession, and forgiveness to keep the lines of communication open. In preparing this material, David was reminded of a recent time when Ike vulnerably shared his hurt and disappointment over missing David's support in a decision he needed to make. Even as it was "scary" for Ike to share this hurt, the relationship deepened through a father-in-law's apology and a son-in-law's forgiveness.

The Fergusons have been known to claim that God has saved the world's best in-laws for their children—and Robin's husband Ike was the first of these gifts. Ike has been just what the "Great Physician" had in mind as his confidence provides security for Robin, and his patience and flexibility temper a certain measure of Robin's "compulsiveness"—possibly inherited from her mom, David might add. Considering that one of God's plans for marriage is to continue our journey in Christlikeness, David and Teresa can rejoice as this work continues in the life of each of these gifts from the Lord—as God provides His new gifts, called son-in-law and daughter-in-law.

Take a revolutionary approach to being a parent-in-law. Seek to understand (unwrap) your son- or daughter-in-law. Imagine what their "Needs List" might look like in terms of what they may have missed growing up, areas where they may have been "undernourished." Then choose to initiate meeting those needs. Rather than reacting, "I can't believe you did that to my daughter . . ." seek instead to look at the "need beneath the deed" and ask the Lord to give you wisdom to discern how you might minister to that unmet need. Enter their world and allow God to use you to fill in some of those gaps.

Grand Relationships!

Grandparents are a tremendous source of blessing. They come in all shapes and sizes, answering to a variety of endearing names such as Grammy and Gramps, Mimi and Papa, and Nana and Popi. It's a sad reality in today's society that most kids don't get to spend much time with grandparents. We barely have nuclear families, let alone extended families. The days of the Waltons are gone. People are spread all over the place. What was true in past generations where extended families maintained close geographic ties and frequent contact is no longer true. This presents new challenges for today's families because children need to feel close to their grandparents.

Whatever side of the grandparenting fence you're on . . . a grandparent yourself or seeking to know how to relate better to your own parents as they grandparent your children . . . consider this word of caution. A grandparent's need to be "needed" is so strong, that if as adult children you don't give them an agenda, they'll find one of their own! It might manifest itself in "correcting" your parenting techniques or going overboard on buying gifts for your children. Give them a need to meet if you don't want them to decide on one of their own. If you are the grandparent, vulnerably share your need to be needed and ask for ways to channel it that will benefit all concerned.

Grandparents have a special opportunity to cultivate in their grandchild that affirmed identity we spoke of in chapter 12 that's brought about by conveying a sense of worth, belonging, and competence.

Worth

A child sitting on a grandparent's lap literally receives a blessing as she is held, touched, and affirmed. Grandparents offer a special brand of warmth and worth. If we could look inside the child's mind, we'd find this process going on: "I know my mom and dad love me . . . because they have to . . . because they had me. But my grandparents live in another city. . . . They don't have to love me. They just do. That's really special. They must think I'm really special!" This communicates to the grandchild that her worth is not based on how much she does or how well she does it but just on the fact that she is who she is! Kids need to hear and feel that.

Grandparents convey a sense of worth to their grandchild as they spend time with him. For grandparents who don't get to see their grandchildren very often, time becomes an even more valuable commodity. Take advantage of the opportunities you do have. When Matthew's "California Grandparents" come to visit, it's clear who they came to see . . . and Paul and Vicky are more than happy to take a back seat. What a delight to see them playing together—morning to night. Whether it's Grandpa and Matthew drawing or watching a football game together or Grandma and Matthew playing board games or cards together, the chemistry is something special to behold. There might as well be a sign hanging around each of their necks that says, "Know what? I think you're special!"

Most grandparents have learned that the secret to joy in

life, just as the Lord has told us, is not in taking but in giving and serving. The greatest thing you can give your grandchild is yourself, but since that's not always possible, give them little things such as cards, pictures, little trinkets to remind them of you. When kids get gifts from grandparents, they have fun with "big-ticket items" for a while, but they keep forever the little things. These *transitional objects* are something they can hold on to that will serve as a connection to the family and the spiritual heritage only you can pass on to them.

Belonging

Grandparents provide living proof that the spiritual heritage they're passing on and the values they cherish really work. Kids can see that even though their grandparents have gone through tough times, they've made it through. This is something kids can only partially learn from their parents because, quite frankly, their parents aren't old enough. They haven't been through enough yet. But as grandparents share memories of their own childhood, how they met, stories about when the child's mom and dad were kids, they are able to look back to generations that have gone before and realize that they are on a generational continuum . . . that their roots go deep.

Several years ago, Matthew's "Oklahoma Grandparents" made an audiocassette recording recounting such memories. Hearing both of his grandparents talk about how they were orphaned at a relatively early age and how God faithfully ministered to them through the difficult times that followed and ultimately brought them together gives Matthew a deep sense of the validity of their faith and appreciation for his heritage.

Belonging to a family with a spiritual heritage is perhaps one of our most important legacies. As grandchildren see grandparents continuing strong in their faith and hear of God's work along the journey, their faith is strengthened and encouraged. Seeing a grandparent give priority to spiritual things says to a child, "You must not grow out of needing God." Powerful impact is made when a grandparent reflects on a testimony of God's working, offers a favorite Bible passage, or vulnerably pauses to pray for a grandchild.

Competence

Grandparents have a unique opportunity to "fill in some gaps" in this area of building competence. While respecting parental boundaries, they can look for opportunities to do things with their grandchildren that the parents either are not skilled in, don't have an interest in, or just don't have time for. This might include things like fishing, gardening, baking pies, or sewing.

Praying for your grandchildren not only gives you a sense of connectedness with them but also enhances their sense of competency. Knowing you're praying that God will empower them to handle certain situations and challenges encourages them to stretch themselves and venture into uncharted territory. There is perhaps no greater motivator than knowing someone is cheering you on through fervent and persistent prayer.

Allow us to interject a challenge for you to consider the opportunities around you for being a "foster grandparent." Whether you have grandchildren of your own or not, there are other children in your sphere of influence who desperately need you. Some may be separated from their biological grandparents by miles, others by death, and still others through the pain of divorce. But whatever their circumstance, they need the affirming love of a grandparent. Don't worry about being "disloyal" to your own grandchildren. You have plenty of love to go around!

Looking at Their Xs and Os

Given the fact that we've all grown up as imperfect people in an imperfect world, there's one thing that is predictable. Your grandchild is growing up in an imperfect family where the parents are imperfectly meeting his or her needs.

Therefore, if you were to do a "Needs Assessment" similar to the one you took in chapter 5, you would see some Os, some half-circles, and some Xs. As a grandparent, you are faced with a fork-in-the-road decision. You can choose to be critical of your children's parenting..."Why don't you do a better job of...." Or, you can view this as an important opportunity for you as a grandparent to help minister to some of those needs by closing some of those half-circles, thereby providing an additional dimension of blessing and balance to your grandchildren.

David's maternal grandfather had just such a ministry in David's life. As he "unwrapped" his grandson and sized up the home situation, he purposefully took an active role in ministering to some of David's unmet needs. David's dad at times was a little too impatient to fish, so David's grand-dad took him fishing. David's dad was a stickler for rules and structure; his granddad, perceiving that he might benefit from a little "flexibility," sought to minister to David's need for unconditional acceptance. No matter the inappropriateness of David's early-teen rebellion, Grand-Daddy Jerry could be counted upon for genuine care and loving support.

As you seek to "fill in gaps," do so with an attitude of respect and support of your grandchild's parents. We're a motley crew—every last imperfect one of us. We all have gaps that need filling in, and it would behoove all of us to aspire to be "gap fillers."

> *Grandchildren are the crown of old men,*
> *and the glory of sons is their fathers.*
> *Proverbs 17:6*

Ask Yourself

1. Take a few minutes and write out the strengths you can identify in your adult child. What gifts and talents has God given her? In what ways has God blessed her? Now with a motive of gratefulness for these strengths, allow God to involve your child in meeting your needs. Are you willing to receive from her? Are you trying to involve your child as your

primary source of emotional support or are you looking to God, and your marriage and to other adult friendships?

2. Consider holidays and times of family get-togethers. Are you encouraging your son or daughter to establish his or her own traditions and schedules? Is there an attitude of flexibility as you try to accommodate schedules with in-laws? Are you welcoming your child as a part of family activities but not demanding that they be at every family function?

3. As you prepare for a son's or daughter's marriage, look for ways to minister to his or her future spouse. Then as you spend time with your new son- or daughter-in-law begin to identify the unmet needs in his or her life. Did he/she miss acceptance? Have you discerned that he/she needs approval? How can you practically meet these needs? Are you fighting the tendency to get angry over the imperfections of your son-in-law's parents? Can you see that an unmet need in a daughter-in-law's life may create conflict for your son?

Experiencing Truth

Philippians 2:3 "Do nothing from selfishness or empty conceit, but with humility of mind let each of you regard one another as more important than himself." Communicate a message of unselfishness to your adult child. Through your words and actions let him know that his marriage relationship is now more important than your relationship with him. Encourage your son or daughter to check with his or her mate before making family plans. Defer to your son and his wife when it comes to financial matters or issues with the grandchildren. Show interest in your daughter and son-in-law's decisions but be careful not to appear intrusive.

Special Thoughts for Single Parents

It may be difficult for you to experience the loss of your own marriage and then be faced with your child's new marriage. Take advantage of time with a journeymate for expressing any hurts or struggles that surface. Show support for your child's marriage and express your hopefulness for their relationship. Reassure your child that he is not leaving you alone. Let him know that God is a tremendous partner and has provided a supportive network of friends. Verbalizing these kinds of thoughts will send a message of relief to your child.

Special Thoughts for Blended Families

You and your partner may have to develop an extra sensitivity and flexibility as you relate to your adult child. The time spent in your home grows even less frequent as they cultivate relationships with in-laws. Focus on what time can be spent together and how to make the most of it. Don't allow a spirit of comparison to rob you of a positive relationship with your son or daughter. Develop an attitude that says "welcome." Your child and her spouse will appreciate the invitation without the pressure. They will want to come home.

EPILOGUE

Practice Hope

AS WE'VE TRAVELED this parenting with intimacy road together, we trust you have been encouraged, challenged, and spurred into action. There is perhaps no higher calling for a parent. There will be days when your heart will be encouraged . . . maybe even jubilant. There will be others when clouds of discouragement will gather. This is our challenge for you — EVERY DAY, PRACTICE HOPE! God has not called you to save the world. He only asks you to be a faithful steward of that part of the world He has entrusted to you. In closing, we'd like to share an experience God used to bring this truth home to Paul several years ago. We'll let him tell the story . . .

"First, let me set the stage. It was a miserably hot summer day on Cape Cod. Quite uncharacteristic! It was during my college days when I was head counselor at a Christian children's camp. We had a group of eight-year-old boys who had been particularly hard to handle. They were in serious need of an 'attitude adjustment.' We decided maybe a change of scenery would help so we loaded them up in the van and headed for the beach. As they piled out of the van, they scattered in all directions. Some headed for the huge sand dunes; others walked out onto the rock jetties that went out into Cape Cod Bay. The jetties extended out into the bay for about a quarter of a mile.

"Picture this . . . we have three adults and about six of these kids crawling around on the rocks acting like little human sea urchins. The adults are standing there with our hands behind our backs, noticing two things. One, it's really hot! I mean, a real scorcher! And humid! We were all miserable. The other thing we noticed is that the tide was completely out. So there was seaweed and sea urchins and snails and starfish laying on the rocks, just baking. You could smell it! We have three cynical adults moaning and groaning about how hot it is and how ornery these kids are. 'Ain't it awful! That seaweed's going to rot; those snails are going to die; the sea urchins are going to bake and shrivel up right before our eyes!' On and on we went. No hope here. Always with our hands behind our backs . . . doing nothing about it.

"Then we heard a voice coming from right below where we'd been standing—and complaining. One of our little human urchins had heard every word we'd said. As we looked down, we saw him picking up little snails, sea urchins, and starfish and throwing them into little puddles amidst the rocks while we were standing there talking about how hopeless it all was. He looked up at us and said, 'Not the ones I'm taking care of! They're going to make it.'

". . . Not the ones you're taking care of. . . . They're going to make it! You're only called to take care of the ones God has entrusted to you. Every day practice hope. The tomb is empty!"

Appendix

Key elements in the **Intimate Life** message include our need for intimacy with both God and meaningful others, our fundamental need to experience biblical truth and God's provision for both our "fallenness" and our aloneness.

Intimacy Principles

1. Man is viewed from a Judeo-Christian worldview as being created in God's image and having existence in three dimensions—spirit, soul, and body. These dimensions give rise to various human functions, namely: the body functions through the five senses and we are "world conscious"; the soul functions through our thoughts, feelings, and choices and we are "self-conscious"; the spirit functions through conscience, intuition, and worship and we are "God conscious."

2. Man is by nature "fallen," separated from God and is motivated out of a need for intimacy with God and intimacy through meaningful relationships ordained by God, i.e., marriage, the family, and the church (the body of Christ).

3. Fulfillment and abundance in life are considered from a biblical perspective as coming by grace through faith in personal intimacy with Jesus Christ and in intimate relationships with meaningful others as ordained by Him.

4. Man's need to relate to Jesus Christ and meaningful others is viewed as a personal challenge to express humility, exercise faith, and experience intimacy. In contrast, man's fallen condition prompts a selfish, self-reliant, and self-condemning response to this neediness.

5. Individual problems in living and relational conflict are considered from an object-relations/developmental framework, in the context of unmet intimacy needs which result in unhealthy thinking, unhealed emotions, and unproductive behaviors. God's concern for both our "fallenness" (Gen. 3) as well our neediness/aloneness (Gen. 2) is considered foundational.

6. This pattern of unmet needs, unhealthy thinking, unhealed emotions, and unproductive behaviors outlines the major hindrances to intimacy and thus the focus of the Spirit's sanctifying work. God is viewed as the ultimate provision for all human neediness and the Bible as giving complete and adequate instruction for mature living and fulfilling relationships.

7. A systems perspective seeks to address the personal, relational, and intergenerational origins of the intimacy hindrances noted above. Thus, in marriage and family relationships, a premise of Genesis 2:24 would be to *"leave father and mother, cleave to one another, and the two shall become one flesh."* In other words, since "leaving " precedes "cleaving," one would expect intergenerational issues to hinder the relational issues involved in marital "cleaving" and these issues to directly impact parenting and family relationships.

8. Intimacy is enhanced through receiving God's manifold grace. His grace is experienced as intimacy needs are met across the spectrum of four major ingredients or intimacy processes, namely: affectionate caring, vulnerable communication, joint accomplishment, and mutual giving. For intimacy to be maintained, these intimacy processes become linked to one another in a repeated spiral over the family life cycle.

9. The family life cycle is considered as bringing predictable challenges to relational intimacy, and thus the need to repeat the "spiral" of intimacy ingredients, beginning with

affectionate caring. Thus, the marital stage of mutual giving is challenged by the addition of children to return to affectionate caring, followed by vulnerable communication, joint accomplishment, and again, mutual giving.

10. Intimacy is built upon man's need to experience biblical truth. The experience of biblical truth leads to emotionally focused freedom, cognitive renewal, and behavioral discipline. The "emphatic comforting of identified hurts and needs" is a pivotal element in the affectionate-caring ingredient of intimacy. Because a fundamental breakdown or hindrance to intimacy results from a lack of empathic comfort, this connection serves as the beginning point of experienced intimacy.

11. A "staged" approach to address individual, marriage, and family issues seeks to address in Stage 1: Initial Assessment (or self-inventory) of the individuals, the marriage and family relationships and the intergenerational dynamics; in Stage 2: Increased Stability of the individual and relationships as a basis for improved functioning and additional maturity; in Stage 3: the Leave-Cleave issues of intergenerational significance which contribute to personal problems in living and relational discord; in Stage 4: the Becoming One Disciplines with both God and others which help ensure relational intimacy, personal maturity, and life fulfillment.

12. A working definition and goal of intimacy in relationships draws upon the biblical model of God "knowing" us, allowing us to "know" Him and His caring involvement in our lives. Thus, mature personality development and fulfilling relationships are based upon this mutual "knowing" and caring involvement.

13. Significant ministry occurs as we serve a God-intended role within the body of Christ to assist and encourage others along a journey toward experiencing "life and life abundant" (John 10:10). Key elements in this ministry in

clude imparting our very life to others (1 Thes. 2:8-9) along with encouraging them to encounter the working of God's Spirit at the point of His Word. Specifically, this ministry role is fivefold as a believer lives and shares biblical truth within the framework of eliminating hindrances and enhancing intimacy. He/she is to assist the individual, couple or family in their need for intimacy with God and with others by:

Eliminating Hindrances

a. Identifying and Interrupting Unproductive Behaviors
b. Resolving Unhealed Emotions
c. Identifying and Countering Unhealthy Thinking
d. Identifying Unmet Intimacy Needs
e. Exposing and Resisting Selfishness, Self-Reliance, and Self-Condemnation

Enhancing Intimacy

Modeling and Reinforcing Productive Behaviors

Experiencing Positive Emotions
Internalizing Healthy Thinking

Modeling and Encouraging the Meeting of Intimacy Needs
Encouraging Expressions of Humility, Exhortation to Express Faith, and Rejoicing in Experienced Intimacy

About the Authors

Dr. David and Teresa Ferguson serve as Directors of Intimate Life Ministries and Professional Associates with the Center for Marriage and Family Intimacy. David's doctoral work at Oxford Graduate School focused on the development of Intimacy Therapy, a biblically centered counseling approach.

David and Teresa appear regularly on the Intimate Life radio program, and have coauthored several books including *The Pursuit of Intimacy, Intimate Moments*, and *Intimate Encounters*. Married for thirty-two years, they are the parents of three children—Terri, Robin, and Eric.

Dr. Paul Warren is the Medical Director of the Child and Adolescent Division of the Minirth-Meier New Life Clinic in Richardson, Texas, as well as a Professional Associate of the Center for Marriage and Family Intimacy. He is the co-author of several books including *Kids Who Carry Our Pain, Things That Go Bump in the Night,* and *The Father Book.* **Vicky Warren,** a graduate of UCLA, has held staff positions with Campus Crusade for Christ, Minirth-Meier Clinics, and *Today's Better Life* magazines before joining the Center for Marriage and Family Intimacy.

Paul and Vicky have been married for fifteen years and have a son, Matthew.

Terri Ferguson is a certified teacher and has taught children of all ages in both church and academic settings. While pursuing an M.A. in counseling, Terri develops curriculum for the Center for Marriage and Family Intimacy and serves as a seminar speaker.